Contents

Contents

Getting into

Veterinary School

James Barton
11th edition

trotman | t

Getting into guides

Getting into Veterinary School

This 11th edition published in 2017 by Trotman Education, an imprint of Crimson Publishing Ltd, 19–21c Charles Street, Bath BA1 1HX

© Crimson Publishing Ltd 2017

Author: James Barton
7th–10th edns: James Barton
5th–6th edns: Mario De Clemente
3rd–4th edns: James Burnett
1st–2nd edns: John Handley (published in 1999 as *Getting into Veterinary Science*)

Editions 1–6 published by Trotman and Co. Ltd

British Library Cataloguing in Publication Data
A catalogue record for this book is available from the British Library.

ISBN 978 1 911067 41 2

Printed and bound in Malta by Gutenberg Press Ltd

About the author

James Barton is Director of Admissions at Mander Portman Wood-ward. As well as being the author of MPW's *Getting into Medical School* and *Getting into Physiotherapy Courses*, James is a sought-after speaker, sits on interview and audition panels, and gives careers advice across a range of fields. He is a regular contributor to the How To Academy and British Council, giving talks on getting into the top universities in the UK. This will be his twelfth Trotman publication.

Acknowledgements

I would like to thank everybody who has contributed to the eleventh edition of *Getting into Veterinary School*. I am particularly grateful to Lianne Carter for her unwavering support, creativity, guidance and, along with many others, for her patience in listening to my animal idioms! I would also like to thank Jade Ramsay, Grace Holmes and Annabel Knowles for their efforts; Melisa Kalkan, Mariella Savage and Becky Parry for their applications; Natalie Wilkinson, Betsy Malamah-Thomas, Guy Beynon and everyone else who contributed to the previous editions of this book. Particular thanks should go to the staff and students at the UK veterinary schools, to Della Oliver and Miranda Lim for overseeing this publication, and to both UCAS and the Royal College of Veterinary Surgeons (RCVS).

Having recently got a dog, I can say that this year, I wrote this book with a new appreciation for the outstanding work that vets do, not only in looking after animals, but also in dealing with the inevitable neuroses of the owners! With that in mind, I also want to acknowledge Duke for all that he does.

James Barton

Introduction
'Do I have a cat in hell's chance?!'

Are you running around like a headless chicken? Champing at the bit? Or are you going about this like a bull in a china shop? Well, the aim of this book is to kill as many birds as possible with one stone. After all, there is truth in the idiom that the early bird catches the worm. The last thing you want is for your application to resemble a dog's dinner or even mutton dressed as lamb, and therefore one cannot over-value the importance of meticulous planning. There's no need to bark at the moon when you can roar like a lion, and this book will show you how to do that. You shouldn't feel like one crow short of a murder were you to take advice here. So, if you feel like a fish out of water and have butterflies in your stomach about the UCAS process, don't despair: this guide is here to help you cope and give you that sense of puppy love and make you the stud of the yard. Remember: stay positive – every dog does have its day. The last thing we want is for you to feel as though there's an elephant sitting on your chest! Relate to the tortoise and not the hare, as last-minute applications are rarely successful. A veterinary school application is all about planning, and although you might find it a bit laborious and that you are repeating things in a parrot-like fashion, these however are indicators that you are probably doing it right. Be dogged in your determination and work like a beaver. If you horse around, feathers will fly. Focus on your own application, don't be catty. No one likes a snake in the grass! That is not to say you shouldn't hunt in packs after you have submitted your application, because after all that is necessary for practice, and a hive mentality can help all involved. If you want to be the queen bee and float like a butterfly, don't be too selective with your choices – a bird in the hand is worth two in the bush.

All right, enough animal clichés for now, but it is important that you note that while the process of applying to veterinary schools will help to shape your future career choice, you should never let it get to the stage where it grinds you down. Aside from anything else, by the end of this book, you should have an answer to the feline question above and be the one who got the cream instead of using up one of your nine lives! And so to business.

About this book

Someone once said to me: 'If you are allergic to animals, being a vet might not be the best career path.' This might sound like a ridiculous statement, but it does make a half-decent point: make sure your career decision is well thought out. In 2015, there were 8,450 applicants (compared to 9,060 in 2014) for pre-clinical and clinical veterinary medicine entry at veterinary school. Of these, 1,195 (compared to 1,085 the previous year) were accepted, a success rate of roughly 15%, and 75 were accepted through Clearing – however, these people most probably already held offers but narrowly missed the grades in the summer exams. For those aspiring to join the veterinary profession, the most important question is 'What can I do to make sure that I am in that 15–20% when I apply?' The aim of this book is to supply you with that information. However, there is no secret formula that will ensure success. The students who are accepted work hard to gain their places. They are motivated and determined, and their desire to work in the field of veterinary science is deep-rooted and genuine. Having said that, without adequate preparation, even the most promising candidate will not get a place if they do not fulfil the required criteria.

This book serves as a guide to help you with the complexities of a veterinary application. Like veterinary surgery, ample preparation is required, alongside an attention to detail, good knowledge, and with all the variables working together.

How to use this book

The competition for places on a veterinary science degree course is ferocious, and the odds of getting in are not as favourable as on other courses. If you look at the University of Edinburgh, for example, they state they receive around 1,000 applications for the undergraduate course and 350 for the graduate entry course. In 2017, 125 places are available, with preferential treatment going to those in Scotland and those paying an EU fee, over an English, Welsh, Northern Irish or international applicant. (After 2017 entry, the picture for EU students is unclear: following the UK's decision to leave the EU, arrangements for EU students studying at UK institutions are to be negotiated as part of formal discussions with the EU.) For another example, for 2015–2016 entry, the Royal Veterinary College (RVC) made 498 offers to 1,507 applicants. As you will see from Tables 1 and 8 (pages 3 and 157), applicant numbers are high. Therefore, you are going to need to prepare thoroughly for this application, taking into consideration all aspects of the course in order to maximise your opportunity of studying veterinary medicine at university.

Table 1 UCAS End of Cycle applicant statistics for Pre-clinical Veterinary Medicine 2007–2016

Year	Total			UK			EU			Non-EU		
	Applications	Acceptances	Ratio of Applications: Acceptances	Applications	Acceptances	Ratio of Applications: Acceptances	Applications	Acceptances	Ratio of Applications: Acceptances	Applications	Acceptances	Ratio of Applications: Acceptances
2016	7,935	1,215	6.5	6,075	995	6.1	1,050	35	30.0	810	185	4.4
2015	8,335	1,165	7.2	6,360	990	6.4	1,160	25	46.4	815	150	5.4
2014	8,965	1,075	8.3	7,170	905	7.9	1,055	15	70.3	740	155	4.8
2013	9,040	1,010	9.0	7,210	825	8.7	1,010	15	67.3	820	170	4.8
2012	8,780	1,020	8.6	7,010	845	8.3	970	15	64.7	800	160	5.0
2011	8,190	970	8.4	6,655	765	8.7	1,010	15	67.3	525	190	2.8
2010	8,150	980	8.3	6,545	780	8.4	1,090	20	54.5	515	180	2.9
2009	7,165	885	8.1	5,860	720	8.1	815	20	40.8	490	145	3.4
2008	6,880	915	7.5	5,675	775	7.3	780	30	26.0	425	110	3.9
2007	6,430	950	6.8	5,340	810	6.6	735	25	29.4	355	115	3.1

Source: www.ucas.com

Notes:

An Application is defined as a choice to a course in higher education through the UCAS main scheme.

Each applicant can make up to five choices, which was reduced from six in 2008. The rule of a maximum of four choices to D1 courses has been in place for the duration of the period covered. The number of applications does not include choices made through the following acceptance routes: Clearing, Extra, Adjustment and RPAs

Acceptance is defined as an applicant who has been placed for entry into higher education.

Pre-clinical veterinary Medicine counts all courses classified by UCAS as 'D1' in the JACS3 subject grouping

This book will discuss all aspects of the application, from how to research and prepare for your application, choosing your course and the application itself, to the interview, results day and information on fees and funding. In Chapter 8 there is advice and information for 'non-standard' applicants – mature students, graduates and retake students. We also look at potential careers within veterinary medicine, and, at the end of the book, there is a further information section and a glossary where you will find details of sources for veterinary medicine and definitions of any abbreviations relevant to your UCAS application for veterinary courses.

The twelve chapters discuss the following:

1. The bare necessities: What is the role of a vet?
2. Horses for courses: Studying veterinary medicine
3. Separating the sheep from the goats: Preparation and experience
4. The 'Jack Russell' Group: Choosing your course
5. Taking the bull by the horns in the cattle market: Applying to veterinary school
6. No one likes a copycat: The personal statement
7. So why did the chicken cross the road? The interview
8. A leopard does not change its spots: non-standard applications
9. A bird in the hand: Results day
10. Counting sheep: Financing your course
11. Snakes and Ladders: Careers paths
12. Don't count your chickens before they've hatched: Further information.

Chapter 1 looks at the fundamentals of being a vet: what is involved, what skills and qualities you need to have and the nature of the work.

Chapter 2 discusses the different types of veterinary medicine course available, focusing on each stage of the degree and looking in depth at the different universities offering this course, analysing what their unique features are for each stage.

Chapter 3 explores the practical aspect of the preparation for an application, i.e. work experience and what each university requires. It looks at the different types of work experience and why such a variety of work experience is required.

Chapter 4 examines further the factors you might wish to consider when choosing a course and the grade requirements for each university.

Chapter 5 walks you through the application itself: admissions tests, deadlines, transferring from one course to another and what to do next.

Chapter 6 is an in-depth look at the personal statement and how it should be written, including what to include and things to avoid submitting.

Chapter 7 discusses the interview stage, possible questions to expect and includes a detailed commentary on topical animal illnesses as noted by the government in 2016.

Chapter 8 addresses international applications, overseas universities, mature students and special educational needs provision in the application process.

Chapter 9 looks at what happens on results day itself and what you will need to do if re-sits are required. It looks at re-applications and gives guidance on what steps you should take next.

Chapter 10 delves into the financial aspects of the course, looking at the cost of veterinary school, including what equipment is required, and then discusses loans and other financing options.

Chapter 11 gives more details about the range of careers you can pursue in veterinary medicine and what you can specialise in after your degree course; accreditation; the importance of people skills and a professional attitude. It then offers a general summation of the application.

Chapter 12 summarises the acronyms used and refers you to other sources of information that you might wish to look at while making an application.

As with other books in this series, including *Getting into Medical School* and *Getting into Physiotherapy Courses*, this book is designed as a guide to the application process as opposed to a guide to the profession. Your work experience is your opportunity to find out more about being a vet.

This book should in no way be seen as dissuasive. It is about getting into veterinary school – it is not designed to put you off and push you towards something else. The tone reflects a balanced mixture of realism and optimism. No one should underestimate the hard road that lies ahead. Getting into one of the eight veterinary schools in the UK (Surrey has now established itself as the eighth) is just the first stage on the route to becoming a qualified veterinary surgeon, with all the inevitable hard work and dedication that will follow in the next 40 years or so. The key to success lies within each individual.

Academic ability is not merely a requirement; it is an absolute necessity. Unless you have the clear potential to study science in the sixth form, this book alone cannot help you. Students attracted to veterinary science should have a natural academic ability in the sciences. A confident prediction of high grades at A level is a great help, but even that will not be enough on its own to get into one of the veterinary schools. You will have to show proof of your interest, enthusiasm and commitment – you will have to show that this is what you really want.

So how do you know that this is the career for you? If you are asking yourself this, your number one priority must be to become well enough informed about and acquainted with the work of a vet to ensure that you have made the right choice of career and to safeguard against regrets further down the line. And once you know this, what do you need to consider next?

- What are the factors involved in choosing a course? Have you considered all of them?
- What do the courses have in common?
- What are the factors that influence admissions tutors to come down in favour of one well-qualified candidate over another?
- What happens at interview?
- What about the various career choices open to the newly qualified vet?
- What do customers who use the services of a veterinary surgeon look for in a 'good' vet?
- Does this sound like the kind of profession that would suit you?

Putting academic skill to one side for a moment, would you feel comfortable dealing with your customers as well as with the animals? The first thing you learn in veterinary practice is that all animals bring an owner with them. How would you handle a sceptical Dalesman or an elderly lady who is anxious and watchful as you come into contact with her beloved pet? Animals play a crucial part in the lives of their owners and whether the vet handles this with tact and understanding will be the deciding factor in both their professional and their personal development. This book will help those who feel drawn to the career for sentimental reasons to understand the realities – good and bad – of being a vet and will enable you to evaluate whether you have what it takes to follow this path.

A feature of this book is real students' views. Many people who are now undergraduates on veterinary courses say that they would have appreciated knowing the views of people in their position when they were at school. Panels of students returning to their former schools to give careers advice often do not include a veterinary student. This book, therefore, includes several student profiles, the first of which is given below.

Case study

Melissa is studying at the Royal Veterinary College (RVC).

'I always wanted to be a veterinarian. In Turkey we have a lot of stray animals and my family and I used to take care of them ever since I was a little kid. This made me grow up with so much love towards animals. This love that I have for animals really kept me going throughout my whole journey to finally get into a vet uni.

'In my personal statement I talked about all the work experience I had done and not only how it helped me understand the whole veterinary world better but also made me grow as a person. I also talked about how I faced some challenges along the way and saw the not so nice sides of becoming a vet (such as, during work experience in Africa, having to put healthy dogs down simply because their owners didn't have enough money to take care of them), and how these challenges have encouraged me – rather than bringing my motivation down – to do more research professionally once I graduate to find better alternatives for the animals.

'The way I prepared for my interview was that I read so much about the common topics (this I feel is a very important thing as in all my interviews they asked me so much about these topics and my experience of/views on them). I had answers prepared for why I wanted to become a veterinarian, as well as why that uni was one of my choices. This sounds quite simple. However, to be able to stand out from others, I actually spent a lot of time preparing my answers.

'I talked about how becoming a vet opens up so many doors, and that I was well aware that it's not only about opening a clinic. I felt they quite liked it when I told them vets could even work for normal human doctors due to zoonotic diseases; work with soldiers for war animals; work in research labs, agriculture, slaughter houses; with psychologists; and everything you can think of, as animals affect many things we don't often think about.

'I also did quite a lot of research as to why that uni was different from all the other ones. This can be in terms of how it structures its course, the facilities it has on campus, different opportunities it can help you with, and so on.

'In all of my interviews I made a few small mistakes that I wish I could go back to and correct. However, I tried not to think about them and move on as soon as possible as I couldn't change what was already done/said and this was only going to affect my other answers in a negative way. I feel like this really helped me.

'During the interviews, I found that even if they ask you an obvious question, they often want you to give more than just the answer to their question. In other words, those questions are there to lead you in a certain way and make you talk about that topic.

'A good example to this was during my Bristol interview. They gave me a scenario where I found an injured badger and they asked me what I would do. To begin with I answered their question by simply saying I would take it to the vet as I wasn't qualified to help them. But then I continued and told them I would also look at what kind of injury it was, and if it looked like a gunshot then I would contact the RSPCA, as during my interview time a new law was introduced for badger culling and people were allowed to shoot them but only if they were locked in a cage, to make sure that they were actually dead instead of suffering. The interviewer said this was a very good answer as I had expanded on more than what they just asked for.

'I applied to Surrey, Nottingham, RVC and Bristol and got an interview from all of them except Surrey. I ended up choosing RVC as my firm choice as I really like the referral hospital there and I thought that was the correct place for me to learn as my goal is to open my own animal hospital after I graduate. Nottingham was my insurance choice because they teach with a lot of practicals and I feel like I learn best that way.

'I got an offer from all of my interviews.

'I did my A levels in one year instead of two as I moved to England the year before the syllabus change. It was a really tough year for me as I was doing three science subjects in a very limited time. I can't count the amount of times I thought I wouldn't make it, but dreaming of my future as a vet kept me motivated.

'I found the easiest way to study was by doing past papers, as after a while I started to understand what each question type was aiming to get out of students. There were some long answer questions that I even learned the mark schemes for as it was just like an exemplar essay answer.

'I was offered AAA but I got AA in my biology and psychology and a B in my chemistry and still managed to get into RVC. This made me fully realise the importance of interviews and personal statements.

'Once I started at RVC, I found that the first week was the hardest as there is a big change in teaching method from A levels to university. I felt like I was constantly confused during my lectures as I was trying to write down everything and this wasn't possible as the lecturers talk very quickly. After a while I started doing prep before my lectures and this was really helpful for me and I gained my confidence back.

'Our lecturers in RVC upload the PowerPoints online before the lecture. What I do is I write down all the learning objectives of the lecture and write down only the relevant parts of the PowerPoint under each of these learning objectives and during the lecture if the lecturer explains something else that is not written in the PowerPoint then I note it down under the relevant learning objective.

'The lecturers keep telling us that we can't possibly learn everything and every single learning objective for any of our exams, unlike A levels. Instead, what we have to do is learn some of them and do further reading about those ones.'

Fact: Almost half the pigs in the world are kept by farmers in China.

1 | The bare necessities
What is the role of a vet?

This is perhaps the most pertinent question of all because the answer to that question reflects the considerable sacrifice in terms of time and effort that every vet makes. Every veterinary practice has to be organised so that someone is on call 24 hours a day, for 365 days a year. As one farmer commented: 'A vet needs to have a really good sense of humour to be called out at 3 a.m. on a cold night to deal with a difficult calving and having to get down in six inches of muck!' It is certainly not a career for someone lacking in confidence, or who holds back and carries an air of uncertainty. Vets are still held in high esteem. The popular image of a vet is of someone working long hours, who is able and caring, whose charges are not too high, and who doesn't worry too much about bills being paid promptly! While this closing sentiment might be ambitious, the popular view is in fact the accurate view.

James Herriot (an English veterinary surgeon and writer) would probably do these words more justice at this stage: he reveals in his books what the profession really entails. In his first book, *If Only They Could Talk*, he reflects on the unpredictability of animals and indeed a vet's life as a whole: 'It's a long tale of little triumphs and disasters,' writes Herriot, 'and you've got to really like it to stick it … One thing, you never get bored.'

On another occasion, Herriot muses, with aching ribs and bruises all over his legs, that being a vet is, in fact, a strange way to earn a living.

> *'But then I might have been in an office with the windows tight shut against the petrol fumes and the traffic noise, the desk light shining on the columns of figures, my bowler hat hanging on the wall. Lazily I opened my eyes again and watched a cloud shadow riding over the face of the green hill across the valley. No, no . . . I wasn't complaining.'*

Some people grumble about the beguiling influence of the Herriot books. There is, however, a lot of cool reality in the pages laden with good humour and philosophy; so much so that one student described the effect of the books as leaving a 'cold afterglow'. Many professions would love to have a PR agent with the skills of Herriot writing on their behalf.

The role of the vet is far more than just scientific curiosity. For large parts, the role of the vet is about education; not only of the self through ongoing continuous professional development (CPD) but, more specifically, of the owners and the public. Prevention over cure in some cases. A lot of animal-based diseases spread very quickly because herds, for example, are often densely packed. As such, it is vital that a vet advises on appropriate animal husbandry, not just with large animals, but within the home as well. An equally important part of the role is to help new pet owners understand the needs of small animals and how to look after them – not dissimilar from understanding how to look after a child for the first time.

CPD is incredibly important throughout your career. The Royal College of Veterinary Surgeons' Code of Professional Conduct for Veterinary Surgeons maintains that, as a practising veterinary surgeon, you have a responsibility to 'maintain and develop the knowledge and skills relevant to your professional practice and competence'; i.e. make sure you are up-to-date for the welfare of the animals ultimately. A minimum amount of 105 hours of CPD over an ongoing three-year period is recommended, with an average of 35 hours per year; though this should always be regarded as the bottom of the scale and the more you do, the more confident you will be that you are fully aware of all developments in the profession.

The choice is fairly flexible, as long as you can justify its purpose. Some examples are:

- discussion group – informal learning set
- practical training – clinical skills lab
- preparing a new lecture/presentation
- research – veterinary business
- secondment to another workplace
- 'seeing practice' – work-based observation
- training – in house.

> 'The best thing about this profession is that it affords so much variety; from domestic to exotic animals, from large animals to birds. You are always learning in this job, and the best way to learn is often to teach – a crucial part of a vet's toolbox.'
>
> Dominic (practising vet in the Wirral)

The principal focus of this chapter is on the role of the vet and what is required in order to make you successful.

So what makes a good vet?

- Confidence
- Authority
- Composure

- Nerve
- Empathy – for both patient and client
- Versatility
- Focus
- Organisation
- Resilience
- Being well informed
- Knowing one's limitations
- Good judgement, e.g. prevention versus cure
- And, above all, a thick skin.

If you have these qualities, a career in veterinary medicine is a strong possibility. Vets are incredibly resilient people who deal with a variety of challenges on a weekly, often daily, basis. You must have confidence in your own abilities and your own judgement, but you must also have the strength to communicate effectively and authoritatively. Bear in mind that you will be calling the shots because you will be the expert.

A good vet can diagnose most things, but, if they cannot, it is their job to know who can. The secret is to know your own limitations. This is particularly important for the newly qualified veterinary surgeon. 'New vets,' according to experienced Cheshire farmer David Faulkner, 'must know when to seek help and be mature enough not to be too embarrassed, for there are always a lot of new things still to learn.'

The farmer's view

'Farmers know immediately if they are going to get on with you,' an experienced vet revealed. 'They look at the way you handle and approach the animals. If you can't catch them, the owner will lose confidence and you won't be allowed anywhere near the livestock.' A seasoned farmer confided: 'Give me a vet who doesn't wait to be asked and is out giving you a hand.' He added: 'If they are confident in what they are doing it soon comes across.' Farmers and animal owners generally like to have a vet who communicates well, has a sense of humour, is outgoing rather than shy and reserved, and is able to walk into any situation and have an answer. There is a stigma about women in the profession and the capability of female vets in large-animal situations. The truth of the matter is that if you choose to specialise in this field (no pun intended), gender issues will disappear if you are confident and firm.

Prevention

Even with the technological advances of the 21st century, prevention makes sense. Animals simply cannot tell you when they are unwell, so a good vet will seek to promote preventive medicine whenever possible. Today there is a lot of knowledge about preventive health by diet and vaccination. Whole herds can be treated at the right time of year. Farmers expect their vet to look ahead and draw their attention to what will prevent disease: 'Look, October is approaching – why not vaccinate all the cattle and prevent pneumonia?' If you give this kind of advice you will inspire faith in those you are seeking to help. Additives can be administered in either feed or drink. This is much better than having to go through the trauma of injecting a whole farmyard of pigs! A vet can do a lot of good with vaccinations and treating deficiencies through the feed by replacing what is not there, improving not only productivity but also the welfare of the animals.

Most people will agree that prevention is better than cure, but sometimes this is a naive statement to make. Preventive medicine is costly, and farmers in particular have a reputation for being frugal. There is no doubt that preventive medicine is a good investment for the future, but in the aftermath of BSE (bovine spongiform encephalopathy), foot-and-mouth disease, and the collapse of much of their export market, farmers are anxious and, in many cases, unwilling to make the necessary outlay. Drug usage for cattle has fallen away. Often farmers do not approach the vet until there is an emergency and by then it might just be an exercise in damage limitation.

In today's busy world, with a general shortage of vets, it is not always easy to respond to this situation. It is said in the profession that you should try to take time to stop and let your eyes range over the flock or herd, looking for the one or two animals that do not fit into the general pattern and who seem out of sorts. There is also a lot to be said for encouraging good husbandry by advising on the housing of the animals. While the sign of a good vet is that he or she will have the latest drug information at their fingertips and knowledge of how to treat certain conditions, sound, informed and diplomatic advice will often earn the vet similar respect and kudos among their clients: 'Instead of me treating the animals' feet, why don't you improve that footpath?'

Small animals

Working with household animals can require a different approach. It is as much about counselling the owners as treating the patients, and, for that reason, interpersonal skills are a prerequisite. With pets, there is great variety: one moment you might be treating a reptile with a nutritional problem; the next, a cat losing weight might be brought in for tests and cause you to wonder if there might be a problem with its liver – or could it be cancer? A rabbit could be brought in – many are now regarded as house pets – and your initial diagnosis of myxomatosis might be confirmed. Or it could be something as mundane as placing a microchip in an animal for security purposes. Dental problems among the small-animal population occur quite frequently but obesity is also much more common than most people imagine. The vet has to advise and persuade the owner – however obstinate they might be – to reduce the animal's feed and bring it in for regular weigh-ins at the surgery.

A lot of animals are kept in busy urban environments, thus increasing the risk of pets being involved in road accidents. If a dog that has been hit by a vehicle is brought in, the 'crash kit' may have to be used. The doses of the most commonly used drugs are marked clearly on the crash box lid, the syringes are loaded, and everything is sterilised and ready. It is important to act quickly, but the true professional keeps calm; this is no time for the vet to fumble when decisive action can save the dog's life.

Arguably the most important quality required for this job is having a thick skin, especially in cases where an animal has to be euthanised. The ethical issues that affect our medical profession and the moral question of 'playing God' do not exist in the veterinary counterpart because it is often kinder to make these decisions for the good of the animal. You have to weigh up the animal's suffering against the owner's protestations and grief and your own conscience. A good vet must find that little bit extra inside themselves. It is crucial to deal with the owners in a compassionate yet effective way. It has often been said that the hope and trust of the owners are matched only by the trust and helplessness of the animals. Imagine dealing with a distraught child when he's told that his pet hamster must be put down. How do you show empathy amid the boy's flood of tears? How do you discuss it with him? Perhaps the boy's parents will let you attempt to explain how the hamster feels and that soon the small animal's pain will cease and the end itself will not be felt. Even when you know it is the kindest thing to do, giving a lethal injection is still one of the toughest parts of the job.

Large animals

The ability to look after large animals is a completely different skill and requires something from you as the vet. Firstly, there is the sheer physicality needed to look after these powerful animals. You cannot be timid around large animals as you need to give them confidence so they trust you.

Then there is the farmer. It is important to note that large animals are the livelihood of the owner and, therefore, dealing with farmers requires a certain diplomacy and resolve from you because, as you can appreciate, they are trying to look at the bigger picture and the impact this might have on business. That is not to say they do not also care about their animals, merely that they have a twin focus which often makes it trickier to advise if you feel a cull is required.

There is also the need for you to see these animals in a different way from small animals. Your job is very much to focus on the health and welfare of the animal, to ensure they are well looked after and that they are not in any danger. That said, you must keep in mind that many of these animals are raised for different purposes, i.e. work and food in the case of most herds. You need to understand this and separate any attachment to the animal out from the job.

> 'Forget about the prejudices towards women and size in this profession; that doesn't matter. However, there is a point behind it in terms of the ability to deal with large animals, therefore my advice is to keep yourself fit. Working outside all the time is very healthy but very cold in the winter!'
>
> Rachel (practising vet in Devon)

So why do you want to be a vet?

It's important to ask yourself this because if you become a vet you will be embarking on a career without riches or glamour. Perhaps for you it is about adapting and fitting into a way of life. Is this what keeps everyone focused during the long hours of study? An interest in and sympathy for animals is taken for granted by many commentators, but in reality it is the way you react to an emergency that puts your dedication to the test. It is all in a day's (or night's) work for a vet and there is no one to applaud you except the grateful, or perhaps less understanding, owner. In short, commitment is the key, particularly if – or perhaps that should be when – the going gets tough. As a vet you must feel that you want to help, cure and take care of animals to the best of your ability, whatever the weather and whatever the circumstances. It is the kind of commitment that will almost certainly have begun at a very early age and will have become stronger and more focused in your teenage and university years. Of course, while the vast majority of qualified vets are in general practice, this is not the only option open to you: you might equally choose to go into teaching, inspection or research. Yet no matter which option you pursue, the level of knowledge and commitment required is very high.

Case study

Percy got his A level results in August 2014 and is studying for a veterinary degree at the University of Liverpool. An early interest in being a vet derived from living on a farm. The daily interaction with animals meant that Percy only had one vocation that he wished to follow. Work experience was easy enough to obtain on the farm but, as he found out, the demands of the university meant that he had to find breadth to this experience.

'Liverpool was very exacting in terms of its requirements for work experience. I had to have a range of both small and large animal experience as well as having observed the workings of an abattoir. This latter work was a real eye opener for me and whilst I, like I am sure most are, was hesitant about this, I understood why, having observed the role of the vet in ensuring the process remains humane.

'The interview was friendly but gruelling but I appreciated that as it made me fight for what I wanted. A bit of lateral thinking never hurt anybody. My mock interview practice was not specific enough for the interview, so I would encourage anyone to research the website thoroughly and try and make contact with people who have already had an interview there. I found online forums incredibly helpful.

'I would also point out that I applied for four universities and only got an interview from one and this seems standard among most students I spoke to, which shows that each university is looking for something different and the one that best matches your skillset will be the one that gives you a chance.

'The thing I think most aspiring vets need to consider is that this is not a glamorous profession; it is about getting your hands dirty and wallowing in the same muck as the pigs. Weather conditions will not affect your outlook and hours will be long, but if you love animals then the rewards are worth the effort.'

Fact: On average, dogs have better – although not as colourful – eyesight than humans.

2 | Horses for courses
Studying veterinary medicine

Given the competitive nature of entry into veterinary school, the idea that there is an element of choice may seem strange. Even when a candidate is fortunate enough to get two or three offers and has to express a preference, the eventual decision is often based on things such as family connections, the recommendation of the local vet or whether or not the candidate liked the school or its location on the open day.

Maybe decisions should be based on more objective data than this, but they seldom are. This might not be a bad thing, as decisions made this way often work out quite well. However, although the courses are not vastly different, it is surely sensible for the candidate to be aware of the typical course structure and what is involved. This could be useful at interview. Most importantly, a knowledge of some of the differences between courses could play a part in your decision, should you get two or more offers.

All the courses leading to a degree in veterinary science have to comply with the requirements of the Royal College of Veterinary Surgeons (RCVS) for recognition under the Veterinary Surgeons Act 1966. This is necessary if the degree is to gain the holder admission to the register, which confers the legal right to practise veterinary surgery. It follows that the courses are fundamentally similar; most of the slight differences come towards the clinical end of the degree. This is quite a contrast to many other degrees, where the differences can be much more marked.

Veterinary courses have a carefully structured and integrated programme with one stage leading logically to the next. This logic is not always apparent to the student, who may feel surprised at the amount of theoretical work in the early pre-clinical stage. Later, as you get into the para-clinical and clinical stages, it all begins to make sense. As one final year student commented: 'It's not until the fourth or fifth year that you suddenly realise "So that's why we did that!" ' In this example, the student was talking about the Molecules in Medical Science first year module, leading into the Mechanisms of Drug Action in the second year, and then the administering of these drugs in the clinical years.

The pre-clinical stage

The first two years are pre-clinical and include a lot of lectures, practicals and tutorials. The normal healthy animal is studied. A basic knowledge of the structure and function of the animal body is essential to an understanding of both health and disease. The scientific foundations are being laid with an integrated study of anatomy and physiology. This study of veterinary biological science is augmented by biochemistry, genetics and animal breeding, as well as some aspects of animal husbandry.

Veterinary anatomy

This deals with the structure of the bodies of animals. It includes: the anatomy of locomotion; cellular structure; the development of the body from egg to newborn animal; the study of body tissues such as muscle and bone; and the study of whole organs and systems such as the respiratory and digestive systems. Studying this subject involves anatomical examination of live animals with due emphasis on functional and clinical anatomy. Students spend a lot of their time examining the macroscopic and microscopic structures of the body and its tissue components. One student said: 'We seemed to look through microscopes for hours at various organs and tissues. At the time it was not easy to see the relevance, but later what we had been doing began to make a lot of sense.' There is not only detailed microscopic study of histological sections but also the study of electron micrographs of the cells that make up the different tissues.

Veterinary physiology and biochemistry

This examines how the organs of an animal's body work and their relationship to each other. This is an integral part of the first two years of the course. It is concerned with how the body's control systems work, e.g. temperature regulation, body fluids, and the nervous and cardiovascular systems. You can expect that your studies will include respiration, energy metabolism, renal and alimentary physiology, endocrinology and reproduction.

Animal husbandry

This extends throughout most courses and introduces the student to various farm livestock and related aspects of animal industries. The kind of performance expected from the different species and their respective reproductive capacities are investigated. Livestock nutrition and housing are studied, together with breeding and management. Students learn about the husbandry of domestic animals and some exotic species. Animal husbandry also involves animal handling techniques. These are important skills for the future veterinary surgeon since the patients will often be less co-operative than those met by their medical counterparts. They may even be much more aggressive than humans!

The para-clinical stage

This is sometimes referred to as the second stage. It follows on from the first two years in which normal, healthy animals are studied. Now it is time to undertake studies of disease, the various hereditary and environmental factors responsible, and its treatment. The third year usually sees the study of veterinary pathology introduced (although it sometimes begins in the second year), with parasitology and pharmacology.

Veterinary pathology

This is the scientific study of the causes and nature of various disease processes. This subject is concerned with understanding the structural and functional changes that occur in cells, tissues and organs when there is disease present.

Veterinary parasitology and microbiology

This deals with the multicellular organisms, small and large, that cause diseases, and with bacteria, fungi and viruses. All the basic aspects of parasites of veterinary importance are studied. Students also take courses in applied immunology (the body's natural defences).

Veterinary pharmacology

This is the study of the changes produced in animals by drugs (artificial defences against disease). It comprises several different disciplines including pharmacodynamics (the study of the mechanism of the action of drugs and how they affect the body), pharmacokinetics (absorption, distribution, metabolism and excretion of drugs) and therapeutics (the use of drugs in the prevention and treatment of disease). Some schools introduce this subject in the fourth year.

The clinical or final stage

The last two years of study build on the earlier years, with food hygiene being introduced, while the study of pharmacology is deepened. The meaning of the phrase 'integrated course' now becomes apparent as all the disciplines come together. Medicine, surgery and the diseases of reproduction are taught by clinical specialists in the final stages of the course, and this part of the course is largely practical. More time is spent at the school's veterinary field station. In some cases you can expect to live at the field station in your final year. Much of the study will be in small groups.

You will be allowed to pursue particular interests; however, the main focus will be on the prevention, diagnosis and treatment, by medical or surgical means, of disease and injury in a wide range of species.

Some practical skills learned in the clinical stage

There are many important practical skills that students have to learn in the final clinical period. One of these is the ability to examine the contents of the abdomen through the wall of the rectum without harming or causing infection to the animal through carelessness. You might also learn to use an ultrasound probe to examine, for example, the ovaries. Another use of ultrasound is to listen to the blood flow and the foetal heart sounds in a pregnant sow. Ultrasound can also assist in carrying out an examination of a horse's fetlock.

Students, like the vets they hope to become, can be called out in the middle of the night to a difficult calving. If a cow cannot give birth naturally, the student can help with a Caesarean operation. Using a local anaesthetic allows the operation to take place with the cow standing, which makes the process easier to manage. Practical skill is also important with foaling. It is best if foaling takes place quickly because it is less stressful for the foal, and students are taught that all that is needed is a gentle but firm pull. Final-year students can assist with lambing, and even with the birth of twin lambs. There are many other examples, too numerous to mention.

General anaesthetic can be used for anything from the full range of horse treatments to vasectomising a ram. Many other techniques are also taught: for example, students might look at images of the nasal passages of a horse and see the nasal discharge from a guttural pouch infection. Another example is learning the right way to trim a cow's foot. All animals (that have them!) can suffer problems with their legs or feet. The experienced veterinary surgeon has to have the skill and confidence to be able to remove a cyst from a sheep's brain without causing a rupture.

No wonder, then, that at this final clinical stage students find that all the earlier preparation comes together and makes sense as clinical problem after problem requires you to think and reason from basic scientific principles. Examples such as these do convey the varied nature of the veterinary surgeon's work, but it is as well to remember that in addition to the physician side of the job there is a lot of routine 'dirty' work. Students have, for example, to help maintain cleanliness in the stables and enclosures of the field station. In due course, when you become a working vet, you may at some stage have to tramp round a muddy farmyard on a cold, wet day carrying out blood tests on hundreds of cattle.

Remember that this summary of some of the clinical work encountered on the course is far from comprehensive and should not lead students to believe that this corresponds to a job description.

Extramural rotation (EMR/EMS)

This is sometimes called EMS (Extramural Studies) or 'seeing practice' and the time is divided between farming work and experience in veterinary practice. Students are required during the first two years to complete 10 to 12 weeks of livestock husbandry, depending on which school they attend. Students usually arrange this experience themselves during their holidays, and on the whole they do not seem to have too much difficulty finding a place. Veterinary schools have lists of contacts in their own area with whom you can get in touch. A modest amount of pay can be arranged directly with the farmer.

During the third, fourth and final years of their course, students must complete approximately 26 weeks of seeing practice. This will be mainly with veterinary surgeons in mixed general practice, with much shorter periods in, for example, laboratory diagnostic procedures and one or two weeks in an abattoir. Casebooks have to be kept and presented at the final examination.

Notes on veterinary courses in the UK

Bristol

A new spiral curriculum based on an integrated structure focuses on the function of healthy animals, followed by looking at the mechanisms of disease and their clinical management. Vertical themes that run concurrently throughout the course will develop students' understanding of the importance of professional skills, animal health and welfare, and veterinary public health.

Students are based in Bristol for the first three years of the course, with at least one day per week spent at Langford, where students will be for the last two years. Some units in years one, two and three are taught by pre-clinical departments that are also responsible for teaching science, medical and dental students. This encourages cross-fertilisation of ideas and access to the latest research findings in other scientific fields. The final year is a lecture-free, clinical year for students to practically develop their training.

Assessment: Mainly by examination, written and computer-based, as well as coursework and oral presentations, normally in January and June each year. Additionally, students are also assessed in DSE (directed self-education) and in practical contributions such as the clinical rotations.

Resits: There is usually a chance to resit all or part of the examination in September if the required standard is not reached in June.

Intercalation: Students may interrupt their studies in year three or four to have a chance to intercalate in a science subject that they have studied, in order to obtain an honours BSc.

Clinical training: The clinical part of the veterinary school is at Langford in the Mendip Hills, about 14 miles outside Bristol. The site hosts a wide range of small-animal, equine and farm facilities including first-opinion practices and referral hospitals. There is also a veterinary laboratories agency and abattoir on site. Students may be placed with leading local practices and farms during their lecture-free final year. The emphasis is very much on small-group clinical rotations. You will undertake 12 weeks of pre-clinical extramural practical experience with animals. These placements are undertaken on farms and other animal units, such as kennels and stables, during the holidays of years one and two. A further 26 weeks of clinical extramural studies (EMS) are undertaken during the holidays of the last three years of the programme. For the most part, the clinical study comprises placements in veterinary practice, but it also includes attendance at an abattoir and optional research placements.

EMS: Bristol is set apart from the other universities as for part of their clinical EMS all students have a 'Foster Practice'. The guidelines recommend that students take 10 to 14 weeks at this practice over the three-year clinical period, so they gain continuous experience. As they say, 'our evidence shows that over the three years they develop in knowledge, skills and confidence. Practitioners and students become familiar with each other, opening greater opportunities for the students to learn and to contribute to the practice.' The type of Foster Practice you will attend, which you choose in your second year, will be based on the variety of experience available to you at your chosen practice, as it is especially important to gain as varied an experience as possible, and it is chosen in the second year. The rest of your CEMS (Clinical Extramural Studies) is up to you, though you have to work within limits: namely, you can only spend up to 10 weeks overseas and six weeks undertaking research. You receive plenty of extra support from the EMS administration office and will be expected to detail this support in the RCVS Student Experience Log when giving your reflections on EMS.

Cambridge

This is the smallest of the veterinary schools. One of its principal strengths is the extensive use the course makes of practical teaching.

The course extends for six years and is divided equally between the pre-clinical and clinical parts. The first three years of the course cover the scientific basis of veterinary medicine in lectures and small-group super-visions; you can expect 20–25 hours of teaching per week. The initial two years are concerned with the basic medical and veterinary sciences, between which there is much common ground at this early stage, bringing you into contact with students from other disciplines. There are also more applied courses in farm-animal husbandry and preparing for the veterinary profession. For the third year, you can elect to study in depth a subject of your own choice from a wide range of options, leading to the award of the BA (Hons) degree at the end of year three. The flexibility of the tripos system is one of its most attractive features. The tripos system is a system in two parts whereby you need to complete both parts in order to achieve an honours degree at Cambridge. Cambridge was the first university to introduce a lecture-free, clinical final year where students work in practice.

There are state-of-the-art facilities on site and there is one of the leading cancer units in Europe, capable of delivering radiotherapy to all sizes of animal. Equally, there is a Clinical Skills Centre with interactive models and simulators that students are encouraged to make use of during their course.

During your pre-clinical studies, students must complete a minimum of 12 weeks of EMS during university vacations.

Assessment: Examinations in the Easter and Summer terms, depending on the year of study, with your progress being reviewed weekly in subject supervisions. Assessment is a mixture of essays, short answers, multiple-choice questions and practical examinations.

Resits: There is an opportunity to resit veterinary examinations in September.

Intercalation: An intercalated degree will be awarded to all veterinary students (not affiliate students). Approximately three years after being awarded, this will be upgraded to a master's degree.

Clinical training: The clinical training course is taught in the Department of Veterinary Medicine at the West Cambridge Campus on Madingley Road. The emphasis is on small-group practical teaching, often eight students in a group, in rotations (or three to four students in some final year rotations). The fourth and fifth years' studies include microbiology, pathology, medicine and surgery. The final year is lecture free with hands-on experience and a period of elective study, and is continuously assessed. The farm-animal practice provides first-opinion clinical services to surrounding farms, including the university dairy farm just a few miles away. A farm-animal referral centre was opened in 2002. Advantage is also taken of the Queen's Veterinary School Hospital (a referral hospital with a full range of modern surgical and medical suites), a nearby Royal Society for the Prevention of Cruelty to Animals (RSPCA) first opinion clinic, specialist equine practices in and around Newmarket and the Animal Health Trust. The department has its own first-opinion practice, an equine referral hospital and equine surgery facilities. During your clinical training, you must complete at least 26 weeks of clinical extramural study during university vacations.

Opportunities for research ensure that veterinary teaching is embedded in the latest cutting-edge discoveries. At the end of the course, those graduating will receive the VetMB membership to the RCVS.

EMS: In the Department of Clinical Veterinary Medicine there is a database of practices that accept Cambridge students and participate in Cambridge's EMS assessment procedure. From this database, students select where they would like to go – they equally have the choice of the National EMS database – and then discuss this with their Veterinary School Clinical Supervisor or the EMS Co-ordinator; the key is balance and variety, all the time remembering that as well as developing your skills, you also have to comply with the national requirement. The expectation is that you spend at least 18 weeks at private veterinary practices within the UK, to include a minimum core requirement of: six weeks' small animal, six weeks' farm animal and two weeks' equine experience.

Edinburgh

Established in 1823, the Royal (Dick) School of Veterinary Studies was the second veterinary school to be established in the UK and the first in Scotland. The 'Dick' school benefits from a collegial community alongside up-to-date techniques. As Edinburgh has American Veterinary Medical Association (AVMA) accreditation, as well as the European Association of Establishments for Veterinary Education (EAEVE), the veterinary degree course (Bachelor of Veterinary Medicine and Surgery or BVMS) gives undergraduate students the opportunity to apply their skills in different countries in the future, whether as a vet or in biomedical research, for example. Edinburgh is internationally recognised for its commitment to excellence through a strong base of research and teaching in a well-supported learning environment. The Easter Bush Campus incorporates a new, purpose-built £40 million teaching building, small-animal, equine and farm-animal hospital facilities with both first-opinion and referral services, and the world-renowned Roslin Institute, located in a new £60 million facility offering opportunities to carry out research supervised by pre-eminent researchers in numerous fields.

As a student, you will also study at Langhill, which is the university's 250-hectare livestock farm. At Langhill, students will learn about animal handling and farm animal medicine. There is also a unique Exotic Animals and Wildlife Service for first-hand experience of dealing with both exotic pets and wildlife commonly found in the UK.

As a result of Colorado State University's status internationally, there is an opportunity for students to study abroad here also.

Assessment: Professional examinations usually include a mix of written and practical components with contributions from in-course assessment, continuous assessment or project work.

Resits: There is an opportunity to resit degree examinations in August if the required standards are not met during the year.

Intercalation: Students with a special interest in animal disease can choose to interrupt their studies and complete a BSc (Hons) in Veterinary Science, usually after year two or three of the programme, which involves one year of advanced study in many different areas including: biochemistry, neuroscience, veterinary biomedical sciences or microbiology and infection. For exceptional students, there is the opportunity to study a one-year research MSc or an intercalated three-year PhD. Students can also enrol on one of the school's prestigious taught MSc programmes, which include Animal Welfare and Behaviour, Infectious Diseases, Conservation Medicine, Equine Science and One Health.

Clinical training: This begins at the start of the first year in the clinically integrated programme with training in examining normal animals across the common species, progressing to abnormal animals in later years. The lecture-free final year emphasises small-group practical, clinical experience where students undertake clinical rotations in the school's hospitals and support services, giving students practical experience in a wide range of disciplines. The final year is longer than the previous years and incorporates an externship and elective periods to allow focus on areas of individual interest. Students also produce a personal and professional development portfolio, which enhances their employability, encourages life-long learning and promotes professionalism.

EMS: The first stage of EMS learning at Edinburgh involves undertaking six weeks of Observational EMS. You will be welcome to start the clinical EMS at any time once you have completed your pre-clinical animal health EMS. This means you will likely be doing Observational EMS between the second and third years in order to experience how a vet practice works as a business. You are expected to be clinically aware by the third year, even though you will have received no training. You then undertake Practical EMS for 20 weeks, for which you can tailor the experience to your interests and career roles, while being realistic in setting objectives and not placing too many demands on practitioners. You will have to complete a portfolio to comply with 'RCVS Day One Competences'. RCVS Day One Competences is a document that sets out the basic and essential competences and skills required by the time you graduate, to ensure that you are safe to practise veterinary medicine on day one of your first job.

Glasgow

Founded in 1862, this is one of the larger schools. It is located at Garscube, four miles to the north-west of Glasgow. The school is considered to be the top in Scotland and the top in the UK, so you will be taught by world-leading professionals. On the site are the pre-clinical and clinical departments, as well as the Weipers Centre for Equine Welfare and a small-animal hospital, and nearby is Cochno Farm and Research Centre, which is used by the university as an additional teaching facility. Some pre-clinical teaching is conducted at the main university campus near the city centre, which enables students to benefit from the opportunities at both sites. The faculty is one of only four veterinary schools in Europe to be accredited to British, European and American standards. In a National Student Survey, Glasgow students reported a 95% satisfaction rating. Delivered in three phases (foundation, clinical and professional) the course follows an integrated structure with vertical themes, placing an emphasis on the skills you will require working as a vet. The final year is a lecture-free year. Glasgow has approved status from the American Veterinary Medical Association (AVMA) and as such, there are plenty of study abroad opportunities.

Assessment: Examination by written and practical work.

Resits: These can take place in September of each year. A second failure may result in repeating a year; normally this is only possible for one year of the course.

Intercalation: At the end of year three, students may study for a one-year BSc (VetSc) honours degree before starting the clinical training. Eight subjects are available. A two-year intercalated BSc honours degree at the end of either year two or year three is another possibility.

Clinical training: The lecture-free final year maximises the opportunities for small-group clinical teaching around domestic animal cases. This takes place at the faculty's busy referral hospital and through EMS undertaken in practices and other veterinary institutions in the UK and overseas.

Special features: As with all UK veterinary schools, every student is expected to complete 38 weeks of EMS in holiday periods. In the first two years students are expected to complete 12 weeks of EMS in the holidays. In the third, fourth and fifth year holiday periods, you are expected to complete 26 weeks of EMS. On the intercalated degree programme students who are in their second or third years of the Bachelor of Veterinary Medicine and Surgery (BVMS) course can elect to come out of the degree and study for an additional qualification on top for one or two years, before re-entering the BVMS programme.

EMS: You are expected to fulfil the 12 weeks' pre-clinical EMS with domestic animal, lambing and dairy farming, as well as six weeks' equine care. After that, your 26 weeks' clinical EMS will start with six weeks' preparatory work. You are advised to experience at least three different types of veterinary work for overall variety to develop your skills and understanding. The remaining time will be Practical EMS of 20 weeks, and this takes place in your latter clinical years. Importantly, you are given flexibility to choose EMS based on what you are interested in and, equally, it will be your responsibility to gain 'RCVS Day One Competences' across a range of species.

Liverpool

This was the first veterinary school to be incorporated into a university structure and therefore the first to establish a university-certified veterinary degree. The Faculty of Veterinary Science celebrated its centenary in 2004. In 2015 it had a 97% student satisfaction rating according to figures on the Unistats website, from the data compiled by the HEFCE (Higher Education Funding Council for England). The principal degree course leading to the Bachelor of Veterinary Science (BVSc) MRCVS, the D100, is a five-year course and students also have the opportunity to incorporate an intercalated BSc. The options for intercalating include a BSc in Conservation Medicine and an MSc in Veterinary Infectious Disease and Control. These courses are also offered to students from other veterinary schools. The faculty also offers a three-year BSc (Hons) in Bioveterinary Science. Teaching on this course is shared between the Faculty of Veterinary Science and the School of Biological Sciences.

Veterinary students spend the first three years of the course on campus in Liverpool studying pre-clinical and para-clinical subjects. The course is modularised. During the fourth and final years, the students are based at Leahurst, the teaching hospital on the Wirral peninsula 18 miles away, which has facilities for equine and livestock cases and a small-animal hospital. First-opinion work (dealing with calls from clients) is undertaken at Fern Grove practice in Liverpool. There are two separate practices operating out of Leahurst, serving the large local equine population and the agricultural sector, and they also get referrals from all over northern England for horses with colic, skin tumours and orthopaedic conditions. Farm visits and investigations extend to the sheep farming areas of north Wales and the dairy farms of Cheshire and Lancashire. Leahurst is in close proximity to Chester Zoo and there is a strong interest in wildlife diseases and animal behaviour.

The university has also established a Foundation to Health and Veterinary Studies Programme (Year 0) with local FE (further education) partners as an access course for those wishing to study a five-year veterinary course, which is typically aimed at mature students and those who have taken a gap away from their studies. You should refer directly to the website for further details.

Assessment: Examination is by both examination and, latterly, practical.

Resits: Resit applications are encouraged.

Intercalation: The veterinary sciences course can be taken with or without an intercalated year.

Clinical training: There is substantial practical work throughout the course. Twenty-six weeks of EMS are completed between years three and five.

Study abroad: Students can currently apply to be part of the Erasmus programme and undertake three-month clinical rotations in years four or five. Opportunities currently exist with the University of Helsinki (Finland), École Nationale Vétérinaire d'Alfort (France) and Vetsuisse (a joint faculty between the Universities of Zurich and Bern, Switzerland). Following the EU referendum result in the UK, UK students applying in 2017 will still have access to the Erasmus+ programme. The UK's future participation in the scheme is to be negotiated as part of wider discussions with the EU.

EMS: Your first two years include undertaking 12 weeks of pre-clinical animal husbandry EMS. As clinical skills have been introduced into Year One, there is an expectation for you to gain some clinical EMS in the first two years of the course. This experience will provide early exposure to the running of veterinary practices as businesses. You then have a requirement of compulsory and choice EMS.

Compulsory PCEMS: lambing, dairy, cattle, horses, pigs, dogs/cats, poultry (one week each).

Compulsory CEMS: public health (two weeks), small animal, farm animal, equine (three weeks each).

Arranging the placements is the responsibility of the student and you must adhere to the EMS requirements. You need to identify and detail your 'learning objectives' before undertaking these placements and then discuss with your EMS placement supervisor.

London

The Royal Veterinary College (RVC), based in Camden Town and Hertfordshire, is the oldest (established in 1791) and largest of the eight UK veterinary schools and the only veterinary school worldwide to be fully accredited by both European (EAEVE) and US (AVMA) authorities, alongside full accreditation with the RCVS and the Australasian Veterinary Board Council (AVBC). This allows graduates to practise in other countries. As one of the University of London's 19 self-governing colleges, the RVC is the UK's only independent veterinary school and it also has a Centre for Excellence in Teaching and Learning. The RVC has developed innovative approaches to learning, and students are equipped with the knowledge and skills needed to succeed throughout their working life. Students spend their first two years undertaking comprehensive pre-clinical studies at the Camden Campus, and then proceed to clinical studies at the Hawkshead Campus in Hertfordshire (north of London).

Assessment: The college uses a wide variety of assessment methods, teaching from a comparative perspective. Some of them are highly innovative and have been pioneered by the RVC. Emphasis is placed on practical work and students are tested by clinical examinations (Objective Structured Clinical Examinations: OSCE), Directly Observed Procedural Skills (DOPS), oral examinations and spot tests as well as written examinations, including multiple-choice questions (MCQs) and extended mulptiple-choice questions (EMQs), problem-solving questions and essay questions.

Resits: A level resits are considered, providing the student achieves the highest possible grade in the second sitting. Resits are also permitted during the course; students are required to pass overall to progress.

Intercalation: Students may intercalate a BSc after successful completion of, normally, the second year. Students can also be considered for certain BSc courses offered by University of London colleges or other universities, or for the RVC's own veterinary comparative pathology course.

Clinical training: In year three, students begin their clinical EMS at a variety of veterinary placements, eventually totalling 26 weeks (up to six of these weeks can be overseas) by the middle of year four. Lectures are timetabled early in the week. On Fridays students get the opportunity to get feedback on their knowledge using the computer-based MCQs. The tutorial system has been revamped recently and students take part in monthly groups of six to eight students. Most of the remaining time is spent gaining hands-on experience in RVC clinics and hospitals (intramural rotations). During year four, students also spend at least eight weeks devising and executing a research project on any aspect of veterinary science that interests them. In holiday periods, there is an expectation for students to complete 12 weeks of placements.

EMS: In order to complete the 26 weeks of CEMS, you are expected to undertake 10 weeks of EMS before clinical rotations start in the second term of the fourth year, with the remaining 16 weeks taking place during clinical rotation. In the first phase, you should see this as preparation work to give you the chance to see how practices really work. The amount of actual hands-on time is limited because clinical skills will not have been learnt yet, but this should be seen as time to understand how a practice operates as a business. In the first period of EMS, students will have to spend at least six weeks at 'three different multi-vet first opinion practices' in the UK, preferably three lots of two-week blocks. You will be encouraged to return to these places during your degree course to further develop your knowledge. The further 20 weeks of your EMS should be used to develop a variety of skills with different animal species. The ideal will be to gain at least two weeks' practical experience with small animals, two weeks in an equine practice, and two weeks in a large animal practice (these should be busy practices to experience working under pressure). The RCVS requires all graduates to be 'a "species omnicompetent" veterinarian regardless of their personal species preferences or future career plans.' RVC students are to attend placements for at least two weeks as it gives more detailed learning; one-week placements are not permitted in the third year. All experience should be made in consultation with your clinical tutor.

Nottingham

Based at the university's Sutton Bonington Campus, Nottingham's School of Veterinary Medicine and Science accepted its first students in 2006. It aims to equip students with all the necessary diagnostic, medical and surgical skills. In 2015–16, the university was ranked third, with 95% in student satisfaction ratings and 100% in graduate employment for veterinary medicine. Its course integrates clinical medicine and surgery with pathology and basic sciences, to ensure that its graduates gain the best possible foundations for a career in the veterinary profession. Studies include time spent at the new, purpose-built clinical teaching facilities and with local clinical practitioners. The five-year degree course leads students from day one through a clinically integrated curriculum and problem-based approach providing learning in all aspects of veterinary medicine and surgery. In years one and two, students undertake a minimum of 12 weeks' animal husbandry EMS, and at least four weeks of clinical EMS in year two. All students undertake a research project in year three, and a minimum of 12 weeks of clinical EMS in both year three and year four. At the end of year three, students graduate with a Bachelor of Veterinary Medical Sciences (BVMedSci). In year four, students will become more accustomed to the business and entrepreneurial skills that are necessary in local practice. The summer term of year four and the whole final year are spent in clinical rotations. This includes a minimum of 10 weeks' EMS. Another 25 weeks of intramural rotations are undertaken in year five, which is lecture free. Intramural rotations may include time at both large- and small-animal practices, laboratory facilities and specialist facilities. After five years of successful study the degrees of Bachelor of Veterinary Medicine (BVM) and Bachelor of Veterinary Surgery (BVS) are awarded.

In addition to the D100 course, there is a D101 course, which includes a preliminary year for those who need to further their knowledge, and a D190 course that includes a gateway year designed for those who need to acquire the scientific knowledge necessary for the profession. You should refer directly to the website for further details.

Assessment: Using different types of assessment, Nottingham aims to measure a wide variety of skill- and knowledge-based learning objectives. There are in-course module examinations including practical tests, essays and short projects. There are also informal assessment opportunities for students to evaluate their progress.

Resits: Applicants will be considered if they resit A levels. Resits during the course are available.

Intercalation: It can be possible to integrate a master's degree into the course.

Clinical training: Each student undergoes as standard 12 weeks of EMS in animal husbandry and 26 weeks overall of EMS in a clinical environment.

EMS: Once pre-clinical EMS has been completed, students undertake a programme of Clinical Extramural Studies (CEMS), which is structured as 20 weeks' student-organised CEMS and six weeks' Vet School-organised 'Formalised CEMS'. This usually starts around the end of Year Two but until the end of Easter in Year Three, students can only undergo a maximum of six weeks so that students gain experiences still whilst realising the need to continue developing their clinical skills. The emphasis for what placements students should take and where is placed on the students, empowering them and forcing them to take charge of their studies, however, they will have access to a database and a support network to help them. They will be allocated a Clinical Tutor and will need to produce an action plan for every placement and make use of the Clinical EMS Handbook given to them during their second year and talks from in-house tutors on getting the most out of CEMS. Placements can be chosen from the database of practices in the Placements Office, along with the RCVS Directory of Veterinary Practices.

Surrey

Based in Guildford, the University of Surrey's is the newest veterinary school and is currently developing year on year. In 2015, a new state-of-the-art, purpose-built School of Veterinary Medicine opened which has plentiful teaching space and includes a world-class veterinary Clinical Skills Centre. The school offers a research-led degree, which provides an interactive environment for learning. More interesting is that the five-year course is designed to create collaborations in animal and human health, with hands-on practical experience from the outset. There is a mixture of taught, clinical and practical work which enables students to fully engage with the material. The School of Veterinary Medicine aims to work alongside chosen veterinary practices to provide students with outstanding experience in general practice and the clinical training required.

A unique aspect of the university is that the veterinary school is currently working with Calgary, Wisconsin, North Carolina and São Paulo Universities as part of the University Global Partnership Network (UGPN). It also works closely with various associations, notably the AHVLA (Animal Health and Veterinary Laboratories Agency), giving the opportunity to develop skills in different areas, such as surveillance, risk analysis and policy.

In accordance with RCVS policy, all students must have 12 weeks of animal husbandry EMS in Years 1 and 2, and 26 weeks of EMS over the following years. There will be a total of 32 weeks of intramural rotations in the clinical year of the course in a wide variety of areas: small-animal practice, surgery, emergency and critical care, veterinary public health, pathology, production animals, equine and electives.

Assessment: The curriculum is arranged to focus on different body systems and integrated horizontally to cover a wide range of subject areas. All aspects of the course are assessed with a range of formative assessments to aid students' work, a portfolio and a skills diary. Formal assessments require all modules to be passed to progress each year.

Resits: Applicants with resits are considered and also those who have applied once before but did not get an interview. However, the school will not consider those who were unsuccessful at interview first time.

Accreditation: Whilst this course does not currently hold RCVS approval for graduates to automatically join the register, it is currently working with the RCVS to ensure that it grants a Recognition Order in 2019.

Clinical training: Students will undertake core clinical rotations as part of the clinically integrated veterinary medicine and science degree. They will also be able to choose from bespoke options to gain unique training in specialist areas, including an option for a research project.

EMS: All students will undertake a minimum of 12 weeks of Animal Husbandry Extramural Studies (AHEMS) in Years 1 and 2 and 26 weeks of Extramural Studies (EMS) after that, in accordance with the RCVS guidelines.

> **Reminder: EMS requirement. To meet RCVS requirements, all students at all veterinary schools must complete 12 weeks of pre-clinical and 26 weeks of clinical EMS, prior to taking their final examinations.**

> Fact: Cows can sleep standing up, but they can only dream lying down.

3 | Separating the sheep from the goats
Preparation and experience

Wanting to become a veterinary surgeon is a long-term commitment. It requires perseverance and a lot of determination. If all goes well and you get the kind of sixth-form science results demanded by all the veterinary schools, it will still take a further five or six years to qualify. Most people faced with the need for intensive study in the sixth form will find it hard to look further ahead than the next test or practical. Yet much more than this is needed if you are to stand a chance of getting into veterinary school.

Starting early

Ideally, the pursuit of your interest in animals and their welfare – in short, your commitment – should have started much earlier than sixth form. There are numerous cases of aspiring vets who have begun their enquiries as early as the age of 12, and certainly many have started gaining their practical experience by the age of 14.

Some vets grew up on a farm and knew that they wanted this kind of life. Others come from an urban background and have developed an interest despite not being brought up in an animal-friendly environment. This interest can be kick-started in a variety of ways and can develop through, for instance, pet ownership, the Herriot books, one of the numerous television programmes such as *Animal Park*, *Super Vets* and *Vet Safari*, or the influence of a friend. 'It's a great life, there's so much variety,' was one student's view. 'You realise it when you start going out getting experience. You see that you can be a vet in a town or in the countryside, that some practices are much larger than others and that some are very busy while others appear more relaxed.'

One young vet said that she had begun her enquiries at about the age of 14 and started working at weekends – her experience began with work in a stables where she began to learn horse riding. Another recalled how she had done kennel work at weekends for four years before becoming a veterinary student. It goes without saying that cleaning out kennels is a dirty, often unpleasant job, and to do this over such a long period shows an impressive degree of commitment and dedication from an early age. Some students have the chance to gain early experience on a nearby farm. But what would you do there? One farmer's wife commented: 'We would expect a 14-year-old to help feed the livestock, to help with bedding-up, which means putting fresh straw in the pens, and sweeping up.' You should be alert to what is happening around you and ask questions: 'Why is that calf coughing? What are you giving it?'

Getting more experience

As those pre-A level years unfold, it makes sound sense to follow up your visits to the local stables, kennels or farm with a week or two spent with your local vet. The point is that you are not just trying to find ways to satisfy the admissions tutor at veterinary school who may one day read an application that you have completed, important though that is; you are also testing your own motivation. This is vital because, make no mistake, you are going to need all the focus you can muster. The task you are about to set yourself is going to draw upon all your commitment, dedication and determination.

It should be pointed out that students who are still at school or sixth-form college will be very lucky to find themselves in the consulting room with the vet. This is because anxious owners will not always appreciate or understand the need for someone of school age to be present. It is much more likely that you will be asked to spend time with the veterinary nurses. As one vet commented: 'Let's see if they can handle animals. Are they frightened?' The idea is to see how the student reacts to aspects of animal husbandry at an early stage. If you cannot abide cleaning up the blood and faeces that go with animal practice, then you should in all probability think of another career. After an artery has stopped pumping or diarrhoea has ended, there is a clean-up job to be done – this is an early experience for many well-intentioned potential vets. Can you take it?

Confirmation of a period spent at a veterinary establishment is one of the conditions for entry to an undergraduate course leading to the degree of Bachelor of Veterinary Medicine or Science. Without getting out and finding out what it is like to deal with sick animals as well as normal, healthy ones, how will you know that you are suited to a career dedicated to providing a service to animals and their owners? As one student put it: 'Knowing what animals look like doesn't necessarily prepare you for what they feel or smell like. There is only one way to find out and that is to get into close contact.' You may think you love animals because of the way you feel about your own pet, but going from the particular to the general may cause you to think quite differently. You might even be allergic to some animals. Make certain that you still feel happy about dealing with animals in general and that you really mean business.

Specific university requirements

Work experience is also vital if you are to have a chance of being called for interview, and without an interview you cannot be offered a place. Some of the veterinary schools are more specific than others about what they expect in the way of practical experience.

- Bristol states that you must show evidence of work experience to justify an interest in the subject, although it is left up to the applicant to acquire as much practical experience as possible prior to interview. What it does require is for you to show that you have worked in a veterinary practice in addition to related work experience at a farm, stable, kennel, rescue centre or abattoir. You will then be tested at interview on your general knowledge gained from your work experience. It also identifies that maximum credit will be given to those who have spent more than four weeks in one particular vet's practice and four weeks across a spread of other experiences. The minimum requirement is one week in both vet and animal establishments prior to submitting the application to it.
- Cambridge is more relaxed about work experience. The Cambridge website states that 'We suggest that applicants should seek to obtain perhaps two weeks of experience shadowing veterinary surgeons in any aspect of their work. We do not specify particular types of practice which must be seen, nor extended periods of work experience, because we believe this would disadvantage applicants who lack the resources to travel to and participate in such work experience.'
- Edinburgh expects applicants to have as much varied work experience as possible. This should be in both small- and large-animal veterinary practices; in livestock farms and dairy farms; in other places, such as zoos, kennels, catteries, wildlife farms and stables; and a day at an abattoir is recommended but not expected. It goes on to say that work experience in a veterinary or biomedical laboratory is also useful. It is not a requirement to complete a particular number of days, and, while breadth is important, your work experience should not be to the detriment of your academic work. Students are required to fill in a Work Experience Summary (WES) at the stage of application.
- Glasgow advises applicants that 'experience working with veterinarians, so that the applicant has some understanding of the duties and responsibilities of a practitioner, is essential before making such a career choice'. They also say that they 'not only assess the breadth of candidates' experience of working with livestock and companion animals, but also examine personal attributes which demonstrate responsibility, self-motivation, a caring ethos and resilience'. They ask you to fill in the Interview Practical Experiences form prior to interview.

- Liverpool requires a minimum of six weeks of work experience relating to the husbandry of a range of animals on a commercial farm or rescue centre, at least four weeks' experience of veterinary practice, preferably spent in more than one practice, and a further six weeks of other animal experience, including farm work, in stables or kennels, etc. Zoo work and visiting abattoirs can be used as work experience but they are not essential. However, experience of UK farming practices is a prerequisite. Students are required to fill in an online Work Experience questionnaire as part of the application by mid-October. This is competitive, and students' work experiences are ranked according to both appropriateness and longevity. There are six categories, including Small Animal husbandry, Equine husbandry, Farm Animal husbandry, 'Alternative' experience (such as abattoirs), Vet clinical experience and Incomplete experience.

- The RVC specifies quality work experience over quantity. It requires two weeks of work experience in a veterinary practice and two weeks in a different animal environment (outside your home environment), such as a kennel, cattery, animal shelter, farm, stables, city farm, pet shop, lambing, wildlife park, zoo, etc. You do not have to have gained experience in all these areas. NB: This is a minimum requirement. You are encouraged to think creatively and experiences should reflect a good sense of the veterinary role in wider society. All applicants must fill in an online work experience questionnaire to support their application.

- Nottingham is fairly open-minded about work experience but requires at least six weeks of animal-related work experience. This could be in general practice, on a farm or at a stables, for example. It will consider references if sent. If you apply to this course, you will need to take the Situational Judgement Test (SJT), which takes the form of an online questionnaire.

- Surrey is asking students to have a minimum of four weeks' work experience with animals and this must include working in a veterinary practice. Work on a farm, in stables, kennels, surgery, research and an abattoir is encouraged. It also requires an official reference from the employer for all work completed prior to the application deadline of 15 October each year.

Making the initial contact

Making the first contact can be quite difficult, often because of your nerves, inexperience or because the vet is cautious and reluctant to take on an unknown commitment. You need to overcome this as soon as possible, because the most proactive students are the ones that get the best work experiences. At the end of the day, the worst anyone can say is no. However, they only want to hear from you, not your parent or guardian. Remember, this is your application, your future and therefore your call to make. It will be seen so much more positively than if your parent calls for you. After the initial approach has been made, the next stage – developing contacts – will seem easy with your growing self-reliance.

Your local vet will know a lot of people through working with animals. A recommendation, or better still an introduction by your local vet to a large-animal practice or a local farmer, may lead to work in a stables or work with sheep, for example. You will get to know people yourself and this will build your confidence.

Developing contacts in this way is known as networking. Taking the initiative like this can do you more favours than always relying on the careers department at your school. However, it is worth checking to see whether your school careers department can help you. Frankly, some school careers departments are much better organised than others. If the careers programme is well organised and planned on an established contact basis, it would be sensible to enlist the department's help. However, do bear in mind that there is concern among some vets that placements organised by schools are not always carefully matched. If you have any doubts on this score, you will be well advised to take the initiative in making your own arrangements.

Remember that in the end it is your own responsibility to get practical experience. Busy people such as vets and farmers are likely to be more impressed with those who exhibit the confidence and self-reliance to make their own approaches.

What the vet will want

Some vets are reluctant to allow young, inexperienced people into their practice. This is understandable. They know that many people are attracted to the idea of becoming a vet; these people have, after all, seen many television programmes! Look at it from the vet's point of view. Some people are attracted to animals for emotional reasons; some may not be academically strong enough to make the grade; some may be so impractical that they could get their finger nipped through one of the animal cages in the first half hour. Do not be surprised if some vets suggest that you should first visit for just a day. The reason for this is that they feel they need to meet you first before committing themselves. As one vet said: 'You can get a fair idea in the first few hours; some are bright and a pleasure to have around.'

What will the local vet ask you to do? This will depend on the vet. 'We cannot afford to waste time so we begin by asking about their capability for science A levels at grades A*, A and B,' remarked one vet. 'We give them three days of blood and gore to see what it is all about. In our case, they will see a farm. We insist on wellies and a good standard of dress, no jeans or open-necked shirts!' Alternatively, your local vet may be a small practice dealing mainly with companion animals – most often cats and dogs, but also rabbits, goldfish, gerbils and budgies. Some students may themselves have gained experience breeding bantams, ferrets, pigeons or fish. This all points to a strong interest.

Some practices are mixed, dealing with farm animals, horses and pets, while in country areas there are practices that deal mainly with farm animals. The types of practice and their size vary widely. The average practice has three or four vets; however, at the one extreme about 2% have more than 10, each with a degree of specialisation, and at the other end of the scale, about 25% are single-handed practices, requiring practitioners to deal with a wide range of work. This being so, the resources that the vet will be able to draw upon will also vary widely.

Shaping up in the surgery

A head nurse in a medium-sized mixed practice uses the following list of questions to enable her or him to judge how students helping in the small-animal surgery are shaping up. They are all well worth considering to make sure you're fully prepared for work experience.

- How keen are they to help in every area? For example, do they clean up willingly?
- How observant are they? Do they watch how we do the bandaging or how we hold the animal straight ready for an injection? Do they watch carefully how we take a blood sample, administer an anaesthetic or set up an intravenous drip?
- Do they maintain a neat and tidy appearance and clean themselves before going in to see a small-animal client? This is very important to the owner.
- Are they friendly towards the client? Do they make conversation and try to establish a relationship?
- Do they ask questions about what they do not understand? They shouldn't be afraid to ask even while procedures are being carried out.
- Are they listening to what is being said and the way it is being said? Do they appreciate the experience that allows the vet to counsel owners on sensitive issues, for example on reducing their favourite pet's diet? This is not an easy message to get across to an overindulgent owner and a vet needs a good 'bedside manner' to be able to tell the owner what must be done without giving offence.

Checklist of experience

Always take up any opportunities that you are offered. Variety of experience will not only broaden your understanding of the profession you seek to join, but will also impress the admissions tutors when they come to scrutinise your UCAS application. Here are some suggestions. Remember, some applicants to veterinary school will have carried out a few of these suggestions four or five years before applying! Others are applicable only to Year 11 or sixth-form students. But if you can tick every box by the time you submit your form in October of your upper-sixth year, well done!

- Get work experience in catteries and/or boarding kennels.
- Work in the local pet shop.
- Make contact with a local vet and indicate your interest by helping with some of the menial tasks. If you are keen you will not mind doing the dirty work.
- Get at least two to three weeks' experience with a large-animal veterinary practice or occasional days or weekends over a long period. Without this, you will not be accepted into veterinary school, no matter how well-qualified you are academically. You must also gain some experience of working in a companion-animal practice. Some candidates are fortunate in having access to mixed practices in which they can gain familiarity with handling large and small animals.
- Visit a local dairy farm and get acquainted with farm work, which accounts for at least 30% of all veterinary science work. Try also to assist on a sheep farm at lambing time.
- Work with horses at a riding stables. (Remember that riding establishments are subject to inspection by an authorised veterinary surgeon.)
- Visit an abattoir if possible.
- Get in touch with one of the animal charities, such as the People's Dispensary for Sick Animals (PDSA) or the RSPCA, and find out about their work.
- Spend a day in a pharmaceutical laboratory concerned with the drugs used by vets as well as medics, or in a laboratory of the Department for Environment, Food and Rural Affairs (Defra).
- Try for any additional relevant experience that may be within your reach, e.g. at a zoo, where you could work as an assistant to a keeper, or in a safari or wildlife park.
- Make a point of visiting local racecourses and greyhound tracks, paying particular attention to how the animals are treated. Perhaps your local vet has a part-time appointment to treat the horses or dogs. If the offer comes to visit with the vet, you should take it.
- Visit country events such as point-to-point races, even if it is only to see what goes on. One day you may get an admissions interview and the more you know about what happens to animals in different situations, the better.

Case study

Wendy was a very diligent student at school. She is in the top third in her year group and increasingly more confident day by day. She worked hard and deservedly achieved the grades she required for university. However, she highlights how much more than just academic attainment is involved in this application.

'I contacted university admission tutors in my first year of A levels as I was worried about not having the work experience to apply for these courses. It was important that I did as it readjusted my strategy going forwards and I would advise anyone to do the same. What I found out was incredibly useful as it enabled me to choose universities based on their requirements. For example, Liverpool was out of the running as I would not have been able to meet their requirements, but I was very encouraged that I could apply to Cambridge as they did not require the same volume. This is not to say I was trying to cut corners – I am at Cambridge now so that is not accurate – but rather I was considering what I could get within the time and how I could balance this with my studies. That was a life skill in itself.

'Growing up in the north of England where animals are part of people's livelihoods, I wrote to as many vets as I could to ask to get a bit of experience, as well as visiting my personal tutor at school to directly ask for his help. I secured three or four placements and was lucky enough to see a wide range of cases, though this was far from easy. I found locating work experience difficult and I encourage anyone to be as proactive as you can in terms of asking people for help; I equally found the time-management aspect tough and there were times when I was not confident of my school work as the temptation was to be distracted by the more exciting work experience. However, this is all part of growing up and with the help of my personal tutor, I was able to become more effective in my second year of A levels.

'Veterinary school is hard work but enjoyable and the skills I learnt early on in my A level career, combined with the proactivity I needed to have, meant that I was in a much better place to understand the profession and what was expected of me.'

Variety and staying power

It is crucially important to demonstrate variety in your practical experience with animals. A visit of just one day to a veterinary practice where you watched small-animal work, followed by another visit to a mixed practice where you were able to see a surgical procedure carried out will be impressive, particularly if you can combine this with work at a stables, some contact with local farms, and at least some experience in, for instance, a kennels. The work experience requirements of almost all universities are stringent and require a significant length of time, therefore isolated days are unlikely to carry the same weight, as it should always be about proving your commitment.

But your application to veterinary school will be enhanced even further if, in addition to this, you can demonstrate a convincing commitment to one or two of the local professionals. What will impress people is the fact that you have willingly returned to your local vet's practice over a period of time, and only the vet will know what it has cost you to do this – and the admissions tutors, of course. True, you will have seen a lot of interesting and varied activities and will have met many interesting people, but many of your friends would have melted away had they been asked and expected to do what you have had to do. Let's face it, not many students would have returned to the practice after having to clean up and deal with blood and muck time and again.

If you can demonstrate both a variety of experience and a committed staying power, there is no doubt that this will count strongly in your favour when the competition for places in veterinary school is at its fiercest.

How to get the most out of your work experience

Work experience is more than just a box-ticking exercise to meet the universities' requirements. It is there to confirm your decision to – or dissuade you from – apply(ing) for this course. You might not enjoy your work experience after all; what sounds like a great idea now might be reimagined after a week on a pig farm getting your hands dirty. The key is to go in with an open mind and be prepared for whatever is thrown at you, and never block a request to assist. You are there to help and to learn.

Try things such as:

- keeping a work experience journal (this may be handy in interviews in the future)
- itemising things that you have enjoyed, things that you have found difficult; essentially, what you did, observations you have, things that inspire you and things you might view as negative. What you are looking for is takeaway points that have helped you make this decision to study the course

- talking to as many of the veterinary staff as possible, not only the veterinary surgeons, but also the reception staff and the veterinary nurses; this is a business after all
- talking to pet owners and get to know them and their animals. How easy do you find it to do so? What struggles does this represent for them and for you? How do you find handling the different animals?

Remember that you are lucky to have the opportunity to get this work experience, so approach it with respect. You will find that you might struggle to get some types of work experience because of disease controls and the regulation of contact with infected animals. However, if you cannot get experience in a particular area, do not be dissuaded; rather, keep trying to get similar experience in another place. You may need to readjust your focus to another type of animal, so be flexible.

Fact: Hummingbirds are the only birds who can fly backwards.

4| The 'Jack Russell' Group
Choosing your course

In order to gain a place at university, you must do your research into all aspects of the course. There is no substitute for preparation. There are only a small number of veterinary schools and therefore there is no excuse for a lack of reading into what the courses entail.

Choice of school

When considering which school to choose, you should look at the course, the teaching style, the applicant numbers and the entry requirements, and you should also visit the university. Studying is an investment, of both time and money, so you must ensure that you can picture yourself at the school for the duration of the course.

Get hold of the prospectuses for these universities. These are free and universities are willing to send them to students. They are also freely available on university websites to download. At the end of the day, the veterinary schools are looking to attract the best students, so they will have marketing material. In addition to these prospectuses, there is also a lot of detailed information on university websites, so you might save yourself a job and find out about courses here. Keep in mind, however, that online information is constantly changing and therefore you might want to keep checking it until you submit your application, to make sure you are up to date about what requirements are expected of you.

Talking to admissions tutors is also an extremely useful exercise when choosing a university. They will be able to answer any specific questions you have, which will help you decide whether you have the best character fit to study there. But **do not** ask them for basic information that you could find out from their website or prospectus. That is a waste of their time and does not reflect well on you.

League tables for veterinary schools reveal only so much, as there are only eight universities offering the specific veterinary medicine course. However, they will tell you about the quality of research, facilities and student satisfaction ratings, important things to consider in the overall university picture.

Open days

You should attend the open days of those veterinary schools that hold special interest for you. Such a visit will give you the chance to see some of the work of the veterinary school. There will be special exhibits, possibly a video programme, and most probably the chance to hear the views of the admissions tutor. There may also be the opportunity to visit the veterinary school's own field station where most of the clinical work is done in the final stages of the course, and although veterinary students are kept very busy you may get the chance to speak to some of them; some schools arrange for a number of their students to accompany parties of visitors on the open day. The open day will also give you an opportunity to see the general attractions of each university as a place to live and study over the next five (or six) years.

As with most things nowadays, everything you need to know is on the internet, so your first point of call must be the individual university websites to look for updated information on their open days. Your school will also receive details of open days, with forms to be completed by those wishing to attend; if you have not heard by about a month ahead of the open day you wish to attend, make enquiries in your school's careers department. If you hear nothing, you should take the initiative yourself and write to the school liaison office or directly to the institution that interests you (see the contact information in Chapter 12). You owe it to yourself to find out as much as you can. Your visit and how you felt about it could be a talking point, should you be called for interview. So do not squander the opportunity to fit one or two visits into your A level study schedule.

If you have already met the academic requirements and are taking time out gaining practical experience, you may be able to attend more open days. If this is the case, you may also find that you receive more than one unconditional offer and so you should certainly try to visit as many of these events as possible to help you make the best decision.

It is a good idea to make notes after each open day of your impressions and what differences you spotted. These notes will be very useful if you are called for interview as you will almost certainly be asked about your visit.

Course entry requirements

The academic requirements of the eight veterinary schools are similar, but there are some differences and it is important that you obtain the most up-to-date information before deciding where to apply. With regard to the course, be very careful that you are selecting the correct option as there are courses with pre-clinical years and Gateway pathways (see Table 2, pages 48–50) that will not necessarily be what you are wishing to study.

You can get information from:

* university prospectuses
* university websites (more likely to be up to date)
* *HEAP 2018: University Degree Course Offers* by Brian Heap (Trotman Education, publishing in May 2017)
* university admissions staff.

Typical student offers for the academic year 2017–18 are listed in Table 2 on pages 48–50.

For A level students, the selectors will take into account:

* GCSE grades (which are just as important as ever without ASs)
* A level choices and predictions or grades
* documentation on any extenuating circumstances that might have affected your performance.

You will be asked for 'good grades at GCSE'. This means lots of grades in the top two bands, particularly in the sciences, English and mathematics. If you did not get good GCSE grades, you can still apply for veterinary medicine, but your referee should make it clear why you did not achieve the grades that you needed – there may have been circumstances, such as illness, that affected your performance. That said, the University of Cambridge has stated in its Admissions Policy for this course that Grade C or above in double award science and mathematics is a minimum requirement, although you should be aware that most students will have higher grades.

NB GCSE and IGCSE examinations are different, with the former switching its grading system in the new reforms, discussed below.

Every university student has to meet the general matriculation requirements of each university (consult the prospectuses for details), but in addition there are the special, prescribed subject requirements. You should check the requirements carefully – the veterinary schools' websites carry the most up-to-date information – but it is likely that you will need three A levels, which will include chemistry, biology and one other science or mathematical subject. Your choice of A level subjects is vital because, although one veterinary school might require two sciences at A level (usually biology and chemistry), others will require three sciences at A level. If you are applying to Cambridge, you should be aware that different colleges have different requirements.

Currently, no veterinary school makes a conditional offer on three A levels at below AAB grades. Unlike the requirements for many other

Table 2 Typical student offers 2017–18

University	A levels required	Preferred grades	Access course available	Access course accepted	Subjects required	BTEC accepted	Widening participation policy
Bristol	3	AAA/AAB (contextual offer; with grade A in chemistry) IB 34 (contextual offer; should include 17 points at Higher Level, including 5 in biology and 6 in chemistry	Yes (BVSc Gateway to Veterinary Science, D108)	Yes – Access to HE Diploma (science or medicine) with at least 30 credits at Distinction including biology and chemistry and 15 credits at Merit	Biology and chemistry (Science practical pass)	Yes – DDD in applied science, animal management or pharmaceutical science, including distinction in science units, and A level Chemistry at grade A	Yes
Cambridge	3	A*A*A+BMAT IB 40–41 with 776 at Higher Level	No	Access to HE Diploma with Distinctions in all relevant subject areas, though Access to HE Diploma alone is not adequate preparation to study a science subject at Cambridge Contact the College admissions office to discuss individual circumstances	Chemistry and two of biology/human biology, physics or mathematics (Science practical pass) See individuall college websites for subject requirements	N/A	Yes
Edinburgh	3	AAA IB 38 to include biology, chemistry and either mathematics or physics at Higher Level and 766 with 7 in chemistry	No		Chemistry and biology and an approved subject (Science practical pass) Good pass in GCSE Physics if not studied at A level	No	Yes

University	A levels required	Preferred grades	Access course available	Access course accepted	Subjects required	BTEC accepted	Widening participation policy
Glasgow	3	A*AA IB 32 with chemistry and biology at Higher Level 6 and physics or mathematics at Standard Level; 6 points minimum in English at Standard Level.	No		Chemistry (A) and biology or either physics or mathematics	No	Yes
Liverpool	3	AAA (with minimum of seven GCSEs) IB 36 with 6 in biology and chemistry at Higher Level	No	Yes – Kitemarked level 3 Access to Medicine with a minimum of 15 credits in biology and 15 credits in chemistry Also run a Foundation to Health and Veterinary Studies programme	Biology and one other science subject If chemistry not offered at A level then it must be a minimum of B at AS (Science practical pass)	Yes DDD with a B in AS Chemistry	Yes
Nottingham	3	AAB/AAB (Vet Med + Prelim Year) and 5 GCSE A grades from a list of subjects IB 34, with 6 in biology and 6 in chemistry at Higher Level and 5 in one other subject	Yes – Certificate in Health Sciences at Lincoln University D190 course is available with a Gateway year		A grades in biology/human biology and chemistry, and B in a third subject (Science practical pass)	N/A	Yes

Table 2 Typical student offers 2017–18 (continued)

University	A levels required	Preferred grades	Access course available	Access course accepted	Subjects required	BTEC accepted	Widening participation policy
London (RVC)	3	AAA/AAB IB at 766 in biology, chemistry and one other subject at Higher Level	Yes – Veterinary Gateway Course		Biology/human biology, chemistry and a third subject (Science practical pass)	Yes	Yes
Surrey	3	AAA/AAB IB 36, with a minimum of 6 at Higher Level including biology and chemistry	No	Yes – including 15 credits (Distinction) each in both biology and chemistry	Biology and chemistry required at grade A Minimum five GCSEs at grade A, including bioloogy, chemistry and physics; English language and mathematics required at grade B (Science practical pass desirable)	N/A	Yes

courses, offers are likely to be made on the basis of A level grades only: stand-alone AS grades are unlikely to be taken into account. However, if you have taken a public exam for your AS at the end of the first year, these grades are important because they will have to be stated on the UCAS application, and thus will give the admissions tutors an indication that you are on course for AAA or higher at A level. For example, when faced with two candidates whose academic backgrounds are identical except that one has AAAA at AS whereas the other has CCCC, who do you think they would favour?

A level reforms

As a result of the Coalition government's review into the state of the education sector, a whole raft of changes were implemented, and these have continued under the current Conservative government. The reforms affect the A level system and the GCSE system. In an attempt to summarise the changes, it is necessary to focus specifically on the impact on students wishing to study Veterinary Medicine, as otherwise the summary could form a whole chapter in itself!

Note that the A level reforms are different in each country of the UK; please see the UCAS website for more details: www.ucas.com/sites/default/files/ucas-guide-to-qualification-reform.pdf. The changes we discuss apply to A levels for students sitting the qualifications set by English examination boards, but there are separate educational reforms taking place in Wales and Northern Ireland (as listed on the UCAS website).

The aim is to move the A level model towards a linear structure, whereby students will sit the full A level at the end of two years. A levels are now linear rather than modular, with assessments mainly by exam, unless another type of assessment is required to test essential skills. The AS and A2 (now historic term) qualifications have been decoupled, which means that the new AS is now a separate qualification and no longer counts towards the A level. Not every school is offering the decoupled AS under the new system. Some schools are offering the option to study a subject at AS as a qualification in its own right alongside the first year of A levels, while other schools are only offering A levels over two years. Most universities have stated that students will not be at a disadvantage if it is not possible to take an AS at their school or college provided they meet the A level requirements, however you should check university websites for their individual requirements.

Changes to A levels in England are being implemented in three phases. In September 2015, Phase One started in art and design, biology, business studies, chemistry, economics, English literature, history, physics, psychology and sociology. The first reformed AS examinations were taken in June 2016 and the first examinations of the full A level will be in June 2017. In September 2016, Phase Two subjects were reformed and the first examination of those will be the AS in June 2017 and the full A level in June 2018. In September 2017, Phase Three subjects will be reformed and examined at AS in June 2018 and the full A level will be sat in June 2019.

In biology, chemistry and physics, practical work will be assessed in two different ways. In the written examinations, your understanding of practical work will be tested, which will account for 15% of the marks and count towards your overall grade. There will also be a separate assessment of your practical skills, although this will be a 'pass, fail' mark, and will be recorded on your qualification certificate. The reforms are not designed to do away with the very necessary practical skills, merely to have them as an ongoing concern, diarised and integrated into the learning as opposed to being standalone tests which benefit some and disadvantage others.

For more information on what will be available for examination in which year of the course up until Summer 2019, visit www.gov.uk/government/publications/get-the-facts-gcse-and-a-level-reform/get-the-facts-as-and-a-level-reform.

Make sure you get the terminology correct:

AS – still exists but is not always required as part of a university offer. No longer counts towards the A level.

A level – there is no such thing as an A2 level any more; an A level tests two years of study in a linear examination.

GCSE reforms

Much like its older sibling counterpart, the GCSE system previously mentioned has been reformed. It is important to note from the outset that it is only GCSEs that have been reformed; IGCSEs have remained the same and are still graded as normal, with letters instead of the new-format numbers in the GCSE system.

One of the main points of this reform is the new grading system (1–9, with 9 being the maximum grade, with mathematics, English literature and English language being the first to present grades numerically in 2017. As with the A level reforms, GCSEs are being reformed in phases; more information of what will be available for examination in which year up until June 2019 is available on www.gov.uk/government/publications/get-the-facts-gcse-and-a-level-reform/get-the-facts-gcse-reform.

As above, the reforms we talk about in this book are predominantly concerning the system in England, while the rest of the UK is undergoing reforms of their own, information about which can be found on the UCAS website: www.ucas.com/sites/default/files/ucas-guide-to-quali-fication-reform.pdf.

The new GCSEs have been designed to give a greater differentiation between all students and mean that the GCSE system can now identify students more accurately in terms of their abilities. Assessment will be mainly by examination instead of coursework. GCSEs are no longer modular and will instead be linear, with assessment at the end of a two-year course. There will still be a foundation and higher tier option to each subject, but only if one paper does not cater for all students. Resits are still available, but only in a November sitting from now on.

There is much ambivalence among universities as to their exact position on the GCSE reforms, with the majority of policy statements suggesting that the importance is not so much on which system is used, rather the choice of subjects studied for breadth of learning will be more crucial. The equivalences of the new grading system to the letter-based system still in operation will vary slightly from place to place, with many universities not having made a decision yet, though the Department for Education is indicating that an A* is likely to be an 8 or 9 and a B is likely to be a 6, though this has yet to be confirmed. Most universities will want mathematics and English language at level 4 or 5 as a minimum requirement.

The A* system

The A* system is a known quantity nowadays and universities increasingly use it as part of their requirements at undergraduate level, normally asking for A*AA. As you can see in Table 2 (pages 48–50), not all universities require an A*AA prediction but you should be aware that a lot of candidates will have this and so the grades that are published should be regarded as a guideline. NB: Cambridge has started asking for A*A*A.

Some students have been known to query whether they should take a fourth A level (not including general studies). Before taking another subject, you should bear in mind that if you offer four A levels your performance in all four subjects will be taken into account. The university particulars themselves will usually say that taking four subjects does not give you an outright advantage. So, if you do feel inclined to add a fourth subject at A level, remember the high grades needed for admission.

Other qualifications

Scottish Highers

For applicants with **Scottish qualifications**, it is likely that you will be asked for AAAAA in your Highers (SCE/SQA) and Advanced Highers in biology and chemistry. Some veterinary schools like candidates to take a new subject at Higher level if only two Advanced Higher subjects are taken in the sixth year. Highers alone are unlikely to be sufficient.

Irish Leaving Certificate

This qualification is accepted at certain universities. It is acceptable on its own or in combination with UK qualifications. It has changed its terminology too (see UCAS Tariff Table on page 158) in 2017 and you will now be expected to get H1, H1, H2, H2, H2, H2 or higher, with H1 in one or both of biology and chemistry.

International Baccalaureate and European Baccalaureate

Another strong sixth-form qualification, the International Baccalaureate (IB) is accepted provided that appropriate combinations of subjects are studied. Three subjects are needed at the Higher level. They must include chemistry and biology, as well as ideally one or both of physics and mathematics. Grade scores needed at the Higher level are likely to be 7, 7 and 6. If the combination is likely to be different, advice should be sought. Similar subject combinations are required by those offering the **European Baccalaureate**. Applicants are likely to need a score of 80% to 88%, including chemistry and biology.

Advanced Diploma

The Advanced Diploma ceased to be awarded from the summer of 2016 and will therefore not form part of an offer.

Access to HE Diploma

Access to HE Diploma must include at least 21 credits at Distinction and 18 credits at Merit and must include biology and chemistry. These must also be Distinctions in all modules taken.

Extended Project Qualification (EPQ)

The EPQ is there to allow students to independently research and analyse a topic of their choosing. It has been designed to promote a learning style that is independent and thorough, helping students identify with a truly undergraduate way of working. The promotion of these skills and values is held in high regard by a university and often carries more weight than an AS qualification, which, as discussed, in itself has lost its value.

In studying an EPQ, students will be able to choose their own topic, be stretched and challenged within that area of research, be largely responsible for their own learning and development and learn new skills, for example, project management and reflection.

The EPQ, for Veterinary Medicine students, can form an interesting basis for discussion at interview. Always remember though, balance an argument if you want to achieve top recognition for it.

The Cambridge Pre-U

The Cambridge Pre-U qualification is becoming more widely understood nowadays as it has been taken up by several leading independent schools. It offers students a different type of qualification for the sixth form, whereby the learning often goes much further, in terms of breadth, and the examining style is more applied, with students requested to apply their knowledge to the questions in a way that most A level syllabuses do not ask of you.

The equivalent Pre-U levels to A level grades are as follows:

Pre-U grade	A level grade
D1	No equivalent A level grade
D2	A*
D3	A
M1	A/B
M2	B
M3	B/C
P1	C
P2	D
P3	E
U	U

It is important to note that the required qualifications differ between all the universities and therefore you should visit the websites to find the most up-to-date requirements.

Veterinary Gateway pathway

The Veterinary Gateway pathway is a one-year course that is part of an extended six-year veterinary degree programme. It was specifically formulated for those students who are part of the UK Widening Participation cohort – a scheme to get more young people into higher education. It is not applicable to international students. The aim of this course is to enable students who have not met the standard entry requirements to develop their skills over the course of an intensive one-year programme.

There are eligibility criteria that you must meet. You must be from a non-selective state school, your parents must not have attended a higher education institution, and your total household income must be £25,000 or less. See www.rvc.ac.uk/undergraduate/vetgateway/index.cfm for more details.

Currently there are Gateway courses at the University of Nottingham, University of Bristol and the RVC.

Checklist

University is about learning, of course, but it is also about the holistic experiences. Remember, university is what you make of it and you have to want to be there after all. It is worth bearing in mind the campus and facilities when making your decision. Think of the distance from home, the distance from the city and the distance from amenities, and make your decision based on these considerations as well. University is as much an experience as it is an academic institution. Try to picture yourself there!

Therefore, consider the following at the application stage.

- Contact all of the universities offering the Veterinary Medicine course and order their prospectuses so that you can compare the offering in each institution.
- Consider the entry requirements as well as the teaching style and the emphasis on practical work and theory.
- Visit the websites of these universities to see if there has been any update to what is in the prospectuses.
- Make sure you visit the universities that you wish to apply to and, if you can, attend an open day so that you can meet members of the department and other students to ask any questions you might have.
- While you are limited in the number of veterinary schools that there are, you should still consider whether you want to be on a campus or in a city, as you will be spending a lot of time studying there and you have to make sure it is right for you. Are you concerned by how far you are from home? Is money a worry for you – if so, you might wish to think about living costs in London versus outside of London (see Table 6 on page 143). If you are a sportsperson, have you considered the available facilities on campus? You should have your own personal shopping list and know your requirements; from accommodation to teaching resources, sports teams to leisure facilities.

- Consider the basic and crucial details, such as location, cost, transport, etc. and how these will affect your budget.
- Consider how far you will have to travel, not only home from your lectures but, if you do not drive, what the implications are with public transport for your EMS.
- Consider the size of the university, the number of students on your course, including the ratio of male to female.
- Research what each university is looking for in its candidates to see if you meet its requirements. If you do not, then you probably want to start arranging the work experience necessary and tailoring your application so you are following the exacting standards set down by the university.
- Research the modules available in each course to make sure that the course will offer you what you want to study.

Fact: A group of owls is called a parliament.

5 | Take the bull by the horns in the cattle market
Applying to veterinary school

Admissions tutors try to get the best students they can for their course. That is putting it at its most basic. But there is more to it than that. They are also acting in the best interests of the veterinary profession. They know that the competition is fierce and that the biggest hurdle faced by aspiring students is entry into a veterinary school. Once this obstacle is overcome, there is, given the undoubted ability of those able enough to get the entry grades needed, every chance that with diligence and lots of hard work the student will in due course enter the profession.

However, it is important to understand that motivation is the key factor in selection. It is, in the last analysis, more important even than A levels or their equivalent. Therefore, admissions tutors look at the total impression conveyed by the candidate in their UCAS application. This will include not only academic predictions and their head teacher's report but also extracurricular interests as well as the extremely important supporting practical experience and references. Admissions tutors know that they are exercising a big responsibility: their decisions will largely shape the future profession.

Taking a broad view

Ideally, admissions tutors will seek to accept students representing a good cross-section of the community. In recent years more women are applying and being admitted than men. Then there is the question of background. Those with an upbringing in country areas can have an excellent range of experience and general knowledge of animal husbandry. Some of them may be the sons or daughters of farmers or vets. Clearly they have a lot to offer. Yet it would be unfair and divisive to fill a course with people who all had these advantages. What of the students coming from the cities where gaining practical experience is not so easy?

A few places will be kept for graduates taking veterinary science as a second degree. There will also be some places reserved for overseas students; they provide valuable income as well as added richness to the mix of students in the veterinary school. Nevertheless, the overwhelming majority of places on these courses will be filled by school-leavers or those who have taken a year out since leaving school.

Academic versus practical

As mentioned in Chapter 3, most veterinary schools require a minimum of six weeks' work experience made up in the way described above. However, despite the strong emphasis on practical experience demanded by all the veterinary schools, many people in the veterinary profession are concerned that the high A level grades required, currently ranging between A*A*A and AAB, suggest that the profession is being filled with people who, while being academically very bright, are not so proficient in dealing with the practical side of the work. Apart from the fact that it is often wrong to assume that academically able people are always very impractical, this trend reveals an imperfect understanding of the logistics of the UCAS operation each year and how the admissions tutors in the veterinary schools deal with it. The UCAS application and the supporting evidence of motivation are crucial to understanding what happens.

Professor Gaskell, when he was Dean of Liverpool's Veterinary School, left no room for doubt that the most important thing from the admissions point of view is understanding what the prospective student is about and his or her motivation. This has to come across in the student's UCAS application. But that is not to say that academic ability is unimportant. There is an enormous amount that has to be learned, and Professor Gaskell advises: 'It's the same with medicine – we find that A levels or their equivalent are good indicators of the ability to absorb, hold and recall information.'

The problem with weaker A levels – and by that we mean subjects such as general studies and critical thinking (though Glasgow goes further to define art, drama, home economics, music and PE, too) – is that you may start to find the amount of learning required at undergraduate level difficult. Fortunately, veterinary medicine is in the position of being able to select the best of the most motivated applicants. It must be added that it is not in the interests of the profession, nor of the animals and owners whom the vets serve, to relax this strong position.

UCAS Apply

Applications for admission to veterinary science degree courses have to be made through UCAS Apply, the online UCAS system. The online

UCAS form is accessed through the UCAS website (www.ucas.com). You register online either through your school or college, or as a private individual. Some of the information that you provide on the form is factual, such as where you live, where you have studied, what academic qualifications you have, details of examinations that you are going to take, and which university courses you are applying for. The final section on the form is the personal statement, where you write about why you want to study at veterinary school and about yourself. We will look at the personal statement in more detail in Chapter 6.

Once your form is complete, it is then accessed by the person who will write your reference; he or she then checks it, adds the reference and sends it to UCAS. After that, you can keep track of the responses from the universities using the online Track facility.

Applications for veterinary science must be received by UCAS by 15 October for entry in the following year. Applications received after this may be considered by the veterinary schools, but they are not bound to do so, and given the number of applications that they will receive, it is likely that they will not do so. In order to ensure that your application reaches UCAS by the deadline, you should complete it at least two weeks before this date so that your referee has time to write his or her report. The current UCAS application form should be available via your school or college. However, if you have left school, or have any difficulties accessing the electronic application system, you should write, after 1 July in the year preceding entry, to UCAS, Rosehill, New Barn Lane, Cheltenham, Gloucestershire GL52 3LZ.

If you are applying to Cambridge, you are required to complete a Supplementary Application Questionnaire (SAQ), in keeping with the requirements of many other universities. More information on applications to Cambridge can be found in another book in this series, *Getting into Oxford & Cambridge*.

Application timeline

The individual stages of the application process will be discussed in more detail in the rest of the chapter. The timeline below shows the tasks that you will need to be aware of over the course of your A level studies and gives an overview of the timing of some of the various things that you should plan for if you are to maximise your chances of gaining entry into a veterinary school.

Year 12

September: Now is the time to be getting work experience. In reality this should have started earlier than this point; however, there is still time and it should be continuous throughout the year in order to meet the criteria of the individual veterinary schools (see page 37). Work experience is a minimum requirement, so do not forget! The best advice is to get some work experience in every school holiday as well as some part-time weekend work in order to meet the requirements.

May/June: Do some serious thinking about the course you'd like to apply to. Get ideas from friends, relatives, teachers, books, etc. If possible, visit some campuses.

June/July: Make a shortlist of your courses.

August: Get your hands on some copies of the official and alternative (student-written) prospectuses, and departmental brochures for extra detail. They can usually be found in school or college libraries, but all the information can also be found by looking at university websites.

Year 13

September: Complete your application online and submit it to UCAS via a referee. It will be accepted from 1 September onwards.

15 October: Deadline for applying for places at veterinary school.

November: Universities hold their open days and sometimes interviews. Entrance examination for BMAT is held.

January: Universities begin to make their decisions and offers will be sent directly to you. If you are rejected by all of your choices, you can use UCAS Extra from 26 February to look at other universities.

2 May: You must tell UCAS which offer you have accepted firmly and which one is your insurance choice if you receive all your university decisions by the end of March. If you receive all decisions by 3 May, you must reply to all offers by 7 June.

Spring: Fill out yet more forms – this time for fees and student loans. You can get these forms from your school, college or local authority.

Summer: Sit your exams and wait for your results.

Early July: International Baccalaureate results.

Early August: Scottish Highers results.

16 August : A level results. UCAS will get in touch and tell you whether your chosen universities have confirmed your conditional offers. Do not be too disappointed if you have not got into your chosen institution; just get in touch with your school or college or careers office. Clearing is not likely to be an option for veterinary courses, although bioveterinary science may appear in August Clearing lists.

As you can see, your main task in your first year of sixth form is to start researching your courses and options, organising and carrying out work experience and then preparing your personal statement. The summer between your first and second A level years should be used to continue building your work experience as well as registering and preparing for BMAT, if you are applying to Cambridge. In the second year, you must hit the ground running, because your UCAS application must be finished by early October and your BMAT will be in early November (check on the BMAT website for the exam date). At the same time, you must also ensure that you stay on top of your studies so you maximise your chances of achieving the A grades you will need, and you should also start preparing for interview and practising your interview skills. Once your final exams are finished at the end of the year, it is simply a matter of waiting for your results so you can see whether you have secured a place.

How many applications to make

You may apply to only four veterinary science courses. If you apply to more than four, your UCAS application will be returned, and by the time you amend it, you may well have missed the 15 October deadline.

A common question is: 'Should I put a non-veterinary science choice in the remaining slot?' While universities cannot see which other courses you have applied to, there are arguments for and against applying to a non-veterinary science course, and you will need to discuss this with your careers adviser or referee. It would probably not be a good idea to apply for veterinary nursing, for example, but it might make sense to apply for a course in equine science. The main point to remember is that you can write only one personal statement and that needs to focus on what you ultimately want to study, veterinary science. This means it will be largely inappropriate for another subject and the admissions staff for that subject will see that you are really interested in veterinary science and so reject you from their course. The admissions staff at the veterinary schools cannot see your fifth choice and so, as long as you don't mention it in your personal statement, it will not affect their judgement. However, you should be wary of putting down a course that you are not interested in and you should try to put down only subjects that are closely related to veterinary science.

Therefore, holding 'insurance' offers will depend on how committed you are to veterinary science. An argument in favour of going all out for the total commitment of applying solely to veterinary schools is that if you fall short of the required grades, and have just missed out, you will almost certainly have the option of gaining entry into an alternative course through Clearing. This is because other pure and applied science courses are invariably much less competitive and you will be able to accept an offer if you want to do so, although it is more likely to be at a lower-ranked institution.

However, if you decide to choose an alternative course as your insurance choice, you should not put down medicine or dentistry. Although admissions tutors will not know what else you are applying for, they will understand you have applied for a different course through your tailored personal statement. Although veterinary science admissions tutors would not automatically exclude anyone because of this mixture, they would certainly look long and hard for overwhelming evidence that veterinary science was what you really wanted. By the same token, you could hardly expect to satisfy the medical and dental admissions tutors!

All things being equal, it seems logical for applications that include a clearly related subject from the D sector of UCAS – which is the sector detailing all animal-related studies, such as agriculture, equine studies, animal physiology, biochemistry, microbiology and zoology – to possess that important quality of coherence and to fit in with the general thrust of the application.

Submitting your application

Once you have completed your application and you are totally happy with it you will need to complete the declaration – found under the 'Send to referee' section of Apply. UCAS cannot process your application unless you confirm your agreement with its terms and conditions, which legally binds you to make the required payment. Remember, by clicking the 'I agree' you are saying that the information you have provided is accurate, complete and all your own work and that you agree to abide by the rules of UCAS.

Checklist

- Personal details: this includes information on you, from your name and address to your fee category status; it also asks if you have given someone nominated access to speak on your behalf – make sure this is someone responsible, such as a parent, guardian or adviser.
- Additional Information: here you are asked equal opportunities questions, as well as the educational background of your parents – make sure you ask for this information first.
- Student Finance (if selected yes): this section will open if you selected '02 Fee' category in Personal Information; at this point you select your borough so that your local authority will send you the correct information.
- Choices: you have four choices and one non-veterinary science choice you can make; most of this section is done through automated lists, though be aware not to accidently select live at home while filling in this section as it is hard to change later if you do not notice you have entered it.

- Education: you need to fill in all relevant education for secondary school level, i.e. the establishments where you took examinations. If for any reason you left a school in this time, you still enter it on to the form for transparency – primary schools are not as important.
- Employment: you should only fill in this section if you have done any paid work; it does not automatically mean the employer will be contacted for a reference.
- Statement: this is your opportunity to sell yourself; you have 4,000 characters including spaces for the personal statement – write it in Word first, although when you copy it across, be mindful of the fact that often the character count may be different because of formatting. Do not worry about spaces in between paragraphs.
- View all details: carefully check through this section and ensure that you have not made any simple errors before submitting the form.
- Payment: agree to all the terms and conditions – you will not be able to submit it if you do not – and then pay by credit card. If you are using your parent's card, make sure you ask first.

Referee's report

After you have completed the declaration, your application is ready to be passed to your referee for completion. He or she will then send it to UCAS. The referee is usually someone who knows you better than anyone else in your school or college, and someone who can draw on the opinions of other members of staff and on information contained in school records. In schools this is most likely to be your form tutor, whereas in colleges it will probably be your director of studies. However, mature students or graduates for whom school was too long ago for such a reference to be meaningful should approach people who know them well. A good idea is to consider asking someone for whom you have worked recently.

References are an important factor since they provide insight into your character and personality. They can also provide significant confirmation of career aims, achievements and interests. The referee's view of your abilities, in terms of analysis, powers of expression and willingness to question things, is the kind of independent information about you that will have an influence with selectors. Additional information about family circumstances and health problems, which candidates rarely offer about themselves, will also be taken into account.

As has already been indicated, performance in A levels (or equivalent exams) is not the sole determinant in selection because of the importance of other motivational factors. However, predicted A level performance is an important aspect for admissions tutors when sifting through and finding committed candidates likely to meet the stipulated academic level. Final decisions are made when A level results are known.

What happens next?

About a week after UCAS receives your application, it will send you a welcome letter and an applicant welcome guide, confirming your personal details and choices. It is vital that you check this information carefully and inform UCAS if there are any inaccuracies. A common mistake is to select the foundation year rather than the start of the course proper, so make sure you haven't done this – for example, someone selecting Veterinary Medicine including a Preliminary Year (D104) at the University of Nottingham instead of Veterinary Medicine (D100) will have two options for a start date: the next academic year or the one after. Be alert and make sure you are selecting the next academic year unless you are taking a gap year or have been advised to do otherwise.

Remember, you will be able to access your application at all times through the UCAS Track system using the same personal ID, username and password that you used to apply.

As soon as UCAS processes your application, your prospective universities can access it, but they will be unable to see the other courses and universities to which you have applied. Once a university has accessed your application, it may contact you to acknowledge receipt of your application; however, not all universities bother doing this, so don't worry if you don't hear from them initially.

Other supporting documentation

Because work experience in veterinary practices and farms is so important in the selection of applicants for veterinary school, you will be expected to list full details of all such experience. Some veterinary schools will send you a questionnaire asking you to expand on the information you gave about work experience in your UCAS application. Applicants can expect interested veterinary schools to follow up by writing to the veterinary practices and farms where you have worked for additional information about you (this information will be confidential). This is a good sign as it shows that your application has aroused more than a passing interest.

In essence, the veterinary school will ask whether the people you have worked with regard you as a suitable entrant into the veterinary profession. The sorts of issues that concern tutors are:

- general enthusiasm
- ability to express yourself clearly
- helpfulness
- practical ability
- attitude to the animals, to customers and to clerical and nursing staff in the practice – in other words, were you a pleasure to have around?

So, it is clear that the veterinary school can take steps to get hold of additional information about you. You can also help yourself by taking the initiative to gain documentary support. For example, once you have received your UCAS acknowledgement and application number, you can ask your local vet to write to the veterinary school(s) of your choice (quoting your application number), giving details of the work that you did there, with extra details of any interesting cases with which you were involved. This information will go into your file and is bound to help, especially if the vet is able to say that he or she 'would like to see this person in veterinary school'.

There are exceptions to this arrangement. For instance, the RVC prefers that you bring copies of all supporting statements, references and casebooks to your interview rather than sending them in advance. It would therefore be wise to contact the individual schools to which you are applying to enquire whether they have any preference regarding how they receive additional statements supporting work experience.

Admissions tests

Applicants to certain medicine, veterinary medicine and related courses are required to take the BioMedical Admissions Test (BMAT). The BMAT is owned and administered by Cambridge Assessment, one of the world's largest assessment agencies. Time is the biggest factor in these admissions tests: there are a lot of questions and you don't have much time to complete them. Of the eight UK veterinary schools, the test is only now required by Cambridge, with Bristol and the RVC removing it from their offers. You may have heard that Cambridge has introduced common-format entrance tests as of 2017 entry (for students applying from September 2016 onwards). However, you should note that the subject test for veterinary medicine at Cambridge will continue to be the BMAT, as in previous years. Details of the test and sample questions are set out on the following pages.

You need to have registered by 15 October and the test takes place in November (you will need to check the BMAT website for the exact date). In 2016 it cost £45.00 for home and EU applicants and £76.00 for international applicants (you should check the website to get the most up-to-date costs). You sit the test at an examination centre, which is often your school; your school will enter you for the test at your request. If you are not able to sit the test at your school, then you will have to find an external centre. Some centres charge an administration fee. There are three sections: Aptitude and Skills; Scientific Knowledge and Applications; and a Writing Task. Go to the website for more details (www.admissionstestingservice.org/for-test-takers/bmat).

1. **Aptitude and skills:** such as problem solving, understanding arguments, data-analysis, critical thinking, logic and reasoning (60 minutes; 35 multiple-choice questions). This tests generic skills that will be useful at undergraduate level. This is split into three sections.

   i. Problem solving: testing your ability to select relevant information and identify analogous cases (marked out of 13).

   ii. Understanding argument: seeing if you are able to identify reasons, assumptions and conclusions and detect flaws in problems (marked out of 10).

   iii. Data analysis and inference: looking at whether you can understand verbal, statistical and graphical information (marked out of 12).

2. **Scientific knowledge and applications:** the ability to apply scientific knowledge from school science to mathematics (30 minutes; 27 multiple-choice questions). You are tested on your core knowledge and whether you have the capacity to apply it. The questions are related to material that would have been included 'in non-specialist school science and mathematics courses'. You therefore have to have a good level of understanding in these subjects. Calculators may not be used. Biology, chemistry and physics all carry 8 marks each and mathematics carries 6 marks.

3. **Writing task:** tests your ability to select, develop and organise ideas and to communicate them in writing, concisely and effectively. You must complete one essay question from a choice of four, which requires you to construct an argument or a debate, analyse a statement or a similar task (30 minutes; one from a choice of four short essay questions). These will include brief questions based on topics of general and medical interest. The questions require you to explain or discuss the proposition's implications, propose counter arguments and identify resolutions. This is your opportunity to demonstrate effective written communication. Marks are awarded based on addressing the question in the way it is required, clarity of thoughts and concise expression.

In Sections 1 and 2, points are scored on a nine-point BMAT scale to one decimal place. The written task is marked by the Admissions Testing Service.

The BMAT is a 2-hour, pen-and-paper test and you cannot use calculators or dictionaries, including bilingual dictionaries, in the exam.

A few sample questions from a Specimen paper are reproduced on the following pages. Additional sample questions are available at www.admissionstestingservice.org/for-test-takers/bmat/preparing-bmat.

Sample Biomedical Admissions Test questions

Try these questions for yourself.

1. Every branchiopod is a crustacean and every crustacean is an arthropod. No insect is a crustacean. Which two of the following statements must be true?

1. Every branchiopod is an arthropod.
2. No insect is an arthropod.
3. No branchiopod is an insect.
4. Some crustaceans are insects.

A 1 and 2
B 1 and 3
C 2 and 4
D 3 and 4

2. The bar chart below shows the reasons for people visiting their family doctors over a 12-month period to the nearest 5%. The chart shows the percentage of consultations due to each problem separately for men and women. The total annual consultation rates are 5,000 per 10,000 men and 6,000 per 10,000 women. The proportion of men and women in the population may be assumed to be the same.

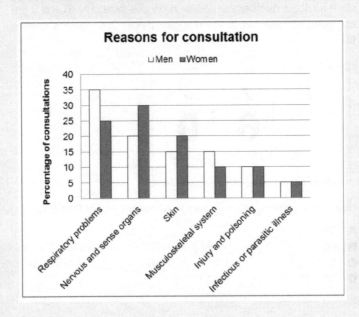

In which of the following pie charts is the proportion of consultations by disease for men correctly shown?

A

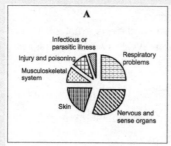

B

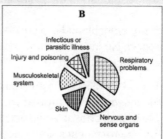

C

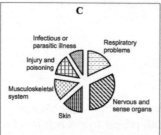

D

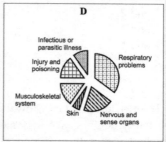

3. A score board has to be able to show and score from 0 to 650. The score is shown by hanging plates on three hooks, each plate having a number painted on it on one side only (6 and 9 are **not** interchangeable). In the diagram below, the score shown is 60.

How many plates are necessary to show any score 0 to 650?

A 25
B 26
C 27
D 30

4. Over the past 100 years there has been a rise in global average temperatures of 0.5°C. Because of this phenomenon of 'global warming' all coastal defences built in the future to protect Britain's most vulnerable regions from flooding should be of a different design to those currently employed, in order to allow for an annual increase in the sea level.

Which of the following are underlying assumptions of the above argument?

1. Global warming is likely to cause a rise in sea levels.
2. The trend of global warming is likely to continue.
3. Current coastal defences are likely to prove ineffective against rising sea levels.

A 1 only
B 1 and 2 only
C 1 and 3 only
D 2 and 3 only
E 1, 2 and 3

From the specimen papers available on the Cambridge Assessment website (www.admissionstestingservice.org). Reprinted by permission of the University of Cambridge Local Examinations Syndicate.

Answers: 1: B, 2: B, 3: A, 4: E

Explained answers and further sample questions are available at www.admissionstestingservice.org/for-test-takers/bmat/ preparing-for-bmat/practice-papers.

The next stage is to wait to hear from the veterinary schools you applied to, once they have considered your application. If you are lucky, the veterinary schools will contact you, asking you to attend an interview. Most veterinary schools wait until all applications are in before deciding who to interview. It is not uncommon for students to hear nothing until after Christmas, so don't panic if you aren't contacted straight away.

UCAS Extra

During the application cycle, if you do not receive any offers in your application, or if you decide that you wish to do something else, you should access UCAS Extra. UCAS Extra gives students a sixth option, though you can only use it if you are prepared to relinquish any offers you hold at the time of accessing it – of course if you have not received any then you will not mind this. It generally operates from late February to early July and contact is encouraged to be made with individual universities which, through the UCAS website, have identified certain courses as being in the UCAS Extra system. You can make as many UCAS Extra applications as you wish but not at the same time, only after you have heard from your previous one.

This is all slightly academic though, because UCAS Extra is highly unlikely to ever apply for Veterinary Medicine. However, it may apply for related subjects and hence the reason for discussion in case you have decided to pursue a different three-year degree. For more information, visit www.ucas.com/ucas/undergraduate/apply-and-track/track-your-application/extra-choices.

What to do if you are rejected

If you are unlucky, you will receive a notification from UCAS telling you that you have been rejected by one or more of the veterinary schools. If this happens, don't despair: you may hear better news from another of the schools that you applied to. If you end up with four rejections, you should take the opportunity to carefully reassess whether veterinary medicine is a realistic career ambition for you and whether there were any parts of your application that let you down. If you still feel that veterinary medicine is for you, take the opportunity to strengthen any aspects of your application that were weak. Under no circumstances should you give up and decide that it is no longer worth working hard; this will only reduce your chances of making a successful application the following year.

Generally, one of the main reasons for rejection is insufficient practical experience, particularly a lack of farm work. If this is true in your own case, you could try to remedy the deficiency between the A level examinations and the publication of the results. All applications are reconsidered after your A level results are known. If your academic results are satisfactory you may be offered a place for the subsequent year.

Some rejected applicants will do better than predicted. When the admissions tutors learn that a rejected candidate has achieved top grades and is excellent in other respects, they have been known to change the original rejection to an unconditional acceptance for the following year. Over 100 places are settled each year in this way. Indeed, the majority of entrants to veterinary science courses will have taken a year out, whether they intended to or not. Those whose grades slip slightly below their conditional offer will usually be considered in August and could be offered entry if places are available. The importance, therefore, of A levels is that once the results are known, the tutors can announce the final decisions that have been made concerning the group of well-motivated and committed pre-selected candidates.

In certain cases, if applicants have met or exceeded the grades asked of them by a veterinary school, they are eligible to enter Adjustment through UCAS. However, it's extremely unlikely that the applicant would be able to find another course in veterinary medicine.

If you are rejected but have reached the necessary academic standard or have narrowly fallen short, you should think carefully before turning away from veterinary science, if that is really what you want to do. There are plenty of cases of people who have persisted and gained the extra practical experience that was needed to tip the scales in their favour. Determination to succeed is a quality that is generally recognised and supported. Think carefully before turning to another science subject. In most cases such a move will prove to be a decisive career choice. This is because it is not possible to transfer from another science course into veterinary school. Nor is it easy to take veterinary science as a second bachelor's degree: graduate applicants have to face stiffer com- petition and the prospect of having to pay high fees if accepted.

Note that going through Clearing is not usually an option for entry into veterinary medicine. Places are limited and often over-subscribed – more offers are made than there are places available, even in a year when the fees increases have led to the government lifting the cap on university places. There can be the odd exception on a year-to-year basis when a few places are available; however, under no circumstances should you bank on any such places becoming available.

Deferring entry and taking a gap year

The UCAS system permits you to apply at the start of Year 13 for entry a year after completion of your A levels. However, you will be expected to meet the conditions of the offer in the year of application. The majority of veterinary schools now welcome students deciding to postpone their entry to the course. The most common reasons given by students are the opportunity to travel, study or work abroad, or to gain additional relevant experience for the course and profession they seek to enter. The latter reason is the one most likely to influence veterinary schools because many applicants do need to strengthen their range of relevant work experience. However, if you are thinking of this, it is better if you wait until you have got your A level grades and then apply in your gap year, as at that point you will have got more work experi- ence, which ultimately is what you need in order to confirm to yourself that this is the right course.

You should be able to explain your plans for the gap year. Do they involve some animal experience? Those coming from urban areas may find that undertaking a gap year of a relevant nature is slightly more difficult to achieve. It is a good idea to discuss this matter on an informal basis with an admissions tutor and get some advice.

Not all of the veterinary schools offer this option. Neither Glasgow nor Surrey accept students who choose this route; the other universities welcome it, especially if it is to gain relevant experience.

Transferring from another degree

If you really want to become a veterinary surgeon, and with hard work you can attain the necessary academic standard, it is not a good idea to take a different degree. Some people are badly advised to do another degree and then try to transfer from another course into veterinary science. However, transferring is not feasible because it is necessary to study certain subjects that are exclusive to veterinary science from the beginning: examples are veterinary anatomy and ruminant physiology. In addition, the chance of there being extra places is remote. Transfer then becomes impossible and the only way you could proceed would be to go back and start your veterinary studies at the beginning. Therefore, no one should be advised to take a different course and then try to transfer. However, it is worth noting that Cambridge has been known to make some concessions to students wishing to transfer from mainly medically related degrees. Such students might, because of the Cambridge tripos system, be able to complete a veterinary science degree at the end of six or seven years' study, depending on when the transfer was made; but they will still need to study veterinary physiology and anatomy.

A further reason why it might prove unwise to do a degree in another subject is that, even if you become a graduate in another cognate subject, with a 2.i or even a First, your application could be assessed on the basis of your original A levels as well as on your subsequent university study. This is done in fairness to the large number of school-leavers applying.

A decisive argument against this route for most people is that, in nearly all cases, graduates in other subjects would be admitted only on a 'full cost' basis. Some colleges allocate a small number of places to graduates within the home and EU intake, but tuition fees for these would usually be at full cost payable throughout the course. There are few to no scholarships available for graduate applicants, with the possible exception of some Cambridge colleges or those that are privately funded, and for these, applicants should refer directly to the university websites.

Fact: Young goats pick up accents from one another.

Case study

Robin studied for a veterinary degree at the University of Bristol. Not necessarily an academic high flyer, Robin worked really hard at school to achieve his grades and gain his place.

'I struggled at school because I knew that everyone else in my class was more capable than me. This spurred me on and made me even more determined to be on a par with everyone else. My interest though lay in the fields with the animals. I spent every weekend working with my local vet gaining experience for this profession. I saw quite a diverse range of animals, from pampered Surrey pooches to hardy bovines and their grizzled owners. This range was crucial as it gave me an appreciation of the variety in the profession as well as indicating to me the pathway I wished to take. I was also very grateful for years of playing rugby as the physical demands of the profession should not be taken lightly.

'I remember clearly on one experience, I got too close to a cow that was in distress. I was young and naive and I got knocked to the ground for encroaching on her space. It was a tough lesson to learn as I was humiliated in front of my employer and the farmer, but it did teach me that you cannot rush into situations. You need to appreciate each animal is different and how to tackle different animals with varying techniques. This was a revelation for me. I stop short of saying I became the horse whisperer but I did learn how to calm an animal down.

'There is very little glamour in this career and the university years are tough. That said, they are incredibly fun and don't be fooled into thinking otherwise. University is what you make of it. My best advice when choosing a course is to consider the type of university you want to be at and let that influence you when picking your four institutions. I would also advise being prepared before the interview. I was fortunate enough to get grilled on bluetongue disease, which I actually knew plenty about, but make sure you are up to date with developments in the profession. What I remember from the people I met throughout my applications is that everyone who applies has similar predicted grades and those you meet at interview will have competitive BMAT results, therefore you need to work out what sets you apart. Are you a shepherd or a sheep and are you more bark than bite? Overusing metaphors, but these are the questions you need to answer.'

6 | No one likes a copycat
The personal statement

Gone are the days of pen and paper. The personal statement is filled in using Apply, the online application system found on the UCAS website, so you can no longer rely on the size of your handwriting to cram in every last possible word. There is a 4,000-character limit (including spaces), which equates to roughly 47 lines. So remember, be concise in what you want to convey and try to be unique.

Importance of the personal statement

The personal statement may be the last part of the UCAS application you fill in, but it is certainly the most important and influential. Most of the information you supply via UCAS is a factual summary of what you have achieved, but in the personal statement you have your first chance to give expression, clarity and style to your application and hence bid for a place at veterinary school.

Make sure you plan your statement carefully. Remember that brevity can often produce a better, more directed answer. Word-process the statement first and then cut it down to within the maximum number of characters if necessary. Research shows that it is a good idea to structure your statement. Some people suggest you consider using subheadings to give clarity for the busy admissions tutor, though it can then look a little bit like a checklist, and you really want it to flow throughout. You may feel it would be better not to use subheadings in the final version; however, by using them in drafts they will give the same structure and inference to the statement, even with them removed. Make sure that the following points are covered in your personal statement.

- Why do you want to be a veterinary surgeon? There are many possible reasons and this is where your individuality will show.
- Outline your practical experience. Give prominence to the diverse nature of it, the clinics, farms, stables, etc. you have worked at or visited.
- Mention any specific interesting cases that you witnessed or assisted with and, importantly, what you learned from them.

- You like animals, but how do you respond to people?
- How did you get on with vets, nurses and the customers? Any teamwork experience?
- Give an indication of your career direction, even if it is tentative at this stage. Show that you have thought about the possibilities.
- Have you had any special achievements or responsibilities connected either with animals or with an outside interest?
- List other activities and interests of a social, cultural or sporting kind. Here is your chance to reveal more about yourself as an individual.
- Finally, remember to keep a copy of your personal statement before you pass it on to your referee. The copy will serve to refresh your memory before you are called for interviews. You need to be prepared to discuss all aspects of your personal statement with the interviewer as they may be using it as a basis to start the conversation. Therefore, and this should go without saying, make it accurate.

The example personal statements below show how an applicant might structure their personal statement. The first example illustrates an old-fashioned but methodical approach to writing a personal statement and will always be useful as a template for your own statement. The other examples are different in their own ways: for instance, the second focuses primarily on work experience, whereas in the third, as well as detailing their work experience, the applicant has also shown an appreciation of different issues affecting vets in practice today.

It is impossible to pick one of these personal statements as the definitive article because they are all individual. There are no right or wrong answers, only a correct template or model to use. As long as the personal statement is personal and means something to you, you will have achieved your goal.

Quotes are desirable in a personal statement only if you can link them to the point that you are trying to make.

> Remember: be concise and try to be unique. This does not mean be extrovert, it just means make it honest to you. How? Relate it back to you and what skills and abilities you can bring to the role and what have you done to hone these skills over time – it may be in different activities and that in itself is original. You are never going to be the same as someone else, though you will have similar work experience because you are following a guideline. Therefore, establish what it is that makes you different and what you really want the university to know about you. Then sell it.

Example personal statement 1 (3,990 characters with spaces)

Our home was like a small rehab centre. Even before knowing that veterinary practice was a profession, I was helping my parents treat sick and injured stray animals. Back then I thought this was the norm never realising that my passion would lead me to something beneficial in the future. My dedication to animals has brought me this far.

When I was old enough to know I wanted to be a vet I started placements, internships and courses, all of which have confirmed my commitment to becoming a vet. Living in geographically and culturally diverse places, such as Turkey, China, South Africa and Sweden, I have come to appreciate the commonalities, regulatory requirements and technical practices and the differences in the profession. My blog www.born-to-be-a-vet.com describes my experiences at vets' surgeries, a university anatomy class, a university farm, a ranch, a cattery, a wildlife reserve and voluntary work.

Volunteering for six months at an international pet hospital and clinics in Turkey, UK and China enabled me to become involved in consultations, clinical case discussions and various surgeries, including castrations, ovariohysterectomies, toe amputation and mass removals, providing invaluable experience. Observing vets analyse test results and write prescriptions taught me the importance of chemistry in veterinary studies. Dealing with emergencies and routine management at a cattery taught me to respond sensitively to delicate situations and empathise with owners prompting my choice of A level Psychology. I am aware of the application of the study of psychology in animal care and welfare, and am acquiring skills and an understanding that will enhance my ability to deliver veterinary medicine.

Working with wild animals at an African game reserve gave me a completely different insight. I experienced a mix of emotions from the satisfaction of helping a hyena return to life to the sorrow of putting young, healthy puppies to sleep, due to financial constraints on the owners, and even using one of them as a cadaver for autopsy. There I witnessed the impact of finances on shelter vets' conditions as opposed to private vets.

Taking the Vetsim and VetMedic courses at Nottingham University I became enthralled not only by the practical and technical elements of being a vet, but also by research, conferences and investigative work, including a genetic engineering session with an opportunity to create my own laboratory species.

During my internship at the research farm of Ankara University, I handled cattle and sheep daily. I also had the chance to be a guest student at the Veterinary Faculty, joining the laboratory sessions and working on cadavers' digestive and respiratory systems, thus realising the importance of studying biology at A level.

I have organised and volunteered in community projects, such as saving new-born sea turtles which showed me how important even one life is for ecology. I am a show jumper and have been riding since I was four. Owning horses and shadowing stable vets for several years taught me how to treat basic illnesses, what to do in emergencies and the importance of prevention techniques. I have several medals for a range of sports, including second place in show jumping at the Longines China Tour. I was also commended by the Chamber of Commerce. Sports and arts have helped in shaping my personality.

As a well-travelled, trilingual young adult, I have had the privilege of living and studying overseas among many cultures which has taught me global tolerance, acceptance and empathy. I am a very sociable and conscientious person with a strong work ethic and an absolute determination to aim high. My ability to work both on my own and in teams as well as in stressful conditions has helped me to pursue my goal of becoming a vet. I cannot wait to conduct research and academic work and participate in clinical and public-health work. For me this is a real opportunity to help animals, their owners and everyone in that community.

Notes on personal statement

- Makes interesting comparisons between working in clinics in different countries.
- Has a variety of work experience.
- Considers A levels here.
- Gives a little context about herself.

However:

- A bit too general in places with her work experience.
- A little too idealistic in places.

Example personal statement 2 (3,983 characters with spaces)

Watching my first dog spay at the age of 14, I was fascinated by the absolute precision of the veterinary surgeon as they skilfully manoeuvred the tissues and delicate vasculature. After this I knew with absolute certainty that the veterinary profession was for me. My desire to strengthen my veterinary knowledge has grown exponentially and I have fully immersed myself in all aspects of the profession.

After engaging in 18+ weeks of veterinary work experience, both locally and internationally, I have a comprehensive understanding of the challenges faced by veterinarians on a daily basis in a wide range of environments. Spending four weeks in various small animal clinics allowed me to observe the intricacies of small animal practice and the importance of inter-personal skills when dealing with clients; for example the delicacy and empathy required in a terminal canine carcinoma case.

During a six-week self-funded placement in a mixed clinic in Ghana I was able to see the opposite end of the scale where financial concerns frequently supersede animal welfare and where the attitude to veterinary care is vastly different. During this placement I was responsible for preliminary checks during consultations, drawing up and helping to administer medication and assisting in surgeries. I was fortunate enough to help close after a hernia repair in a sheep by performing several simple interrupted stitches. Assisting in an ear cropping surgery reinforced the ethical concerns associated with this practice. The need for problem-solving skills was imperative for making the most of limited resources, for example when making a make-shift cast out of masking tape and a swab sample tube for a two-week-old kitten with a suspected fractured leg.

I learnt to appreciate how vets contribute to human health by ensuring the quality of our meat and milk while balancing the needs of the farmer with concerns for the animal's quality of life during several weeks spent lambing and on a dairy and poultry farm. A day at an abattoir fortified this. I thoroughly enjoyed the hands-on nature of lambing and I admired the fast-thinking of the farmers in critical situations. During a week on the road with a farm vet I observed an emergency bovine caesarean, assisted in a difficult pygmy goat birthing and helped with de-horning 60 calves.

A week on the road with an equine vet and another at a specialist equine hospital taught me about the intricacies of metabolic disorders and diagnostic options when dealing with lameness. I was also able to observe a suspensory ligament neurectomy. A week at a stud farm enhanced my understanding of the care of elite sports horses and introduced me to the complexities of breeding. Having owned my own horses I am very comfortable in an equine environment, and competing at national level has taught me discipline, dedication and teamwork. I worked as a riding instructor at a riding stables for several years where I developed my leadership and communication skills.

Additionally, during a week at a zoo I learnt about the importance of nutrition and intellectual engagement of wild species.

While participating in my Duke of Edinburgh Gold Award and during regular meetings as a charity rep at school I developed a passion for volunteering and charity work. I volunteered at a school in Kenya where I was responsible of a class of 20 pupils for six weeks. On my return I have raised £2,000 and have independently set up a 12-month renovation project, which has reinforced the importance of organisation and perseverance.

At university I have volunteered and fundraised for Guide Dogs and attained my Level 1 My Guide certificate. I am also a STEM Ambassador whereby I travel to disadvantaged schools to engage children in scientific activities and help them broaden their horizons. This will be a valuable experience for explaining diagnoses to families as I'm well practised in explaining scientific terms in a way children can understand. I am also an active member of the biology, snowsports and art societies and this year I hope to participate in CommuniTea, a student-led association that organises tea parties for elderly people in care homes, as well as becoming a zoology specimens volunteer.

Key modules in my biology degree, such as parasitology and immunology have allowed me to draw interesting parallels across human and veterinary medicine, while statistical and bioinformatics modules have advanced my mathematical and analytical problem solving skills.

I am enthusiastic, self-motivated and dedicated to the veterinary profession. I believe my strong problem-solving skills and intellectual curiosity make me very suitable to this dynamic career and I look forward to performing my first dog spay.

Notes on personal statement

- A very good level of relevant work experience.
- Includes a variety of experiences and, importantly, what was learnt from them.
- Shows commitment.
- Shows an understanding – and value – of research.

However:

- A little too narrative in places.
- Starts to read a little like a shopping list when the zoo is mentioned, and that paragraph could have been further developed to illustrate the difference between the types of animals cared for in a zoo versus those in a small veterinary practice.

Example personal statement 3 (3,965 characters with spaces)

I knew before secondary school that I wanted to be a vet and when I started doing a variety of work experience and pre-vet courses I began to see how much would be involved – hence my work experience blog: in_vet_erate@livejournal.com. When my two-year-old guinea pig developed a growth I became intrigued by the vet and all he had to say. My work experience began there when I was 14: first during the school holidays, then a three-week summer job in 2009, when I was trusted to restrain animals while the vet took blood, gave injections and inserted catheters. I have had ongoing paid work there as a weekend kennel hand since January 2010, going in when they are closed to feed and, if necessary, medicate boarding cats. Other vet experience includes a week at a rural small-animal practice and four days with a large-animal vet. Highlights for me in these contexts were correctly recognising a case of feline diabetes and being guided to perform rectal examinations on several cows.

Two days at an abattoir showed me aspects of the meat industry. It provided an excellent anatomy lesson and a glimpse into pathology. Three days at a vet laboratory gave a different slant on this and I learned to do blood smears and separate serum from blood.

I have had varied farm experience: two weeks on a dairy farm, two days of lambing and a week at a large pig farm. On these farms I delivered lambs, drenched them, gave bottle feeds and docked tails, and with the pigs I gave injections, cut teeth and performed AI (artificial insemination) on several sows. Even more interesting was working for a week on a buffalo farm (herd of 200). I was intrigued by these more 'wild', less domesticated animals and that consequently mastitis and digital dermatitis are less common. I was very involved in all the tasks in the milking parlour, including giving oxytocin injections.

I attended Vetsim and Vet-Medlink, VetCam and VetQuest, the Embryo Vet School course and 'An Introduction to Farm Animal Management' at Harper Adams UC. These courses linked satisfyingly with my work experience, where I saw theory in practice. They were a fascinating glimpse into the diversity and challenge of veterinary medicine and I have been eager to go on all I could. Completing an ILM Level 2 course in Effective Team Member Skills at school made me more aware of effective team working, both on farms and in vet surgeries. On Bronze and Silver Duke of Edinburgh expeditions I enjoyed the humour and support that comes from teamwork, and on work experience I enjoyed pulling together to milk a large herd and for a busy night of lambing.

I relish challenges: I enjoy grappling with a problem and gain immense satisfaction when I arrive at a solution. Developing skills is also satisfying: playing the violin and recorder to Grade 8 (increasing my motor skills); being logical and methodical with mathematics but also open to the possibility of a solution sliding out of the blue. History has improved my academic skills of essay writing and being analytical. In chemistry there is the problem-solving factor and also interesting chemical processes, such as homeostasis. I especially enjoy biology and have completed papers on bluetongue disease and also, from an extra day at Vet-Medlink, a paper on nanotechnology, which I passed with merit.

Responsibilities at school that tie into my interests include helping the junior school orchestra and volunteering as a student librarian. I love to read, whether novels or the Veterinary Practice journal – the articles detailing procedures are particularly fascinating and may be useful in the future. I also enjoy ballet and tennis, learning Mandarin and cross-stitch, which will hopefully be useful for suturing.

I am very self-motivated, with a great enthusiasm for veterinary science. The opportunity to work with a vast range of species and the numerous skills that are required as a vet are prospects that I find very exciting and I eagerly look forward to the challenges I will face.

Notes on personal statement

- Includes a reference to the student's blog – admissions tutors do say to include a link to a blog (if you have one) if you want a way to provide them with more information.
- Some good examples are given.
- Talks about current studies.
- Mention of some manual dexterity.

However:

- Mentions a lot of work experience but not much depth to the discussion about it.
- Could include more detail on the Vetlink courses.

Example personal statement 4 (3,974 characters with spaces)

From a young age I have had a deep interest in animals, which was encouraged by my holiday job on a poultry farm since 2003, yet it was not until recently that I seriously considered veterinary science to be a viable career option. Throughout my time at school I was guided towards engineering; however, I was never really certain that it was what I wanted to do. I therefore rejected my five engineering offers part way through my gap year, in order to apply for veterinary science.

During my gap year I worked with a wild game vet in South Africa on private game farms and hunting lodges all over the country, capturing, transporting and supervising the general care of the animals. As a result of this I began for the first time to look at becoming a vet. Upon my return to the UK I began a week's work experience with my local vets in Sussex in order to investigate the more typical side of veterinary work. It was invaluable to be able to see the day-to-day side of veterinary work. This ranged from small-animal surgery to dealing with some of the more difficult clients. One incident that stands out was an eye enucleation, my first real experience of surgery. Aside from the fascinating surgery, it was wonderful to see the dog a few days later, once the swelling had subsided, and he was returning to normal. I also accompanied vets on their large-animal visits, helping with tuberculosis testing and debudding in cattle, and attempting a few pregnancy diagnoses of my own. It was interesting to see the differences in approach between working with animals in the UK and in South Africa: in general I found that in the UK the processes of diagnosis and treatment had a much greater emphasis on science, as opposed to the 'patch and go' system when working with wild game. I have been able to continue working there over the last few months.

Alongside this, I have worked on a dairy farm, in a stable and an animal rescue sanctuary. On the dairy farm I worked as a labourer and was involved in all aspects of farm work, from mucking out to milking. I learnt a great deal while I was there, in particular relating to the prevention and treatment of mastitis and milk fever, which I was surprised to see being carried out by the farmers, rather than the vets, illustrating the practical rather than theoretical side to the treatment. My week at the stables was brilliant; I arrived with very little experience of horses, and after that week I now feel confident in horse handling. It was a busy week, with visits from the vet, the farrier and the dentist, and I watched them all with interest. Especially noteworthy was a case of thrush that developed from a split in the frog of a shire horse, and as my week came to an end we could see a decrease in lameness. As a result of this work experience I am now absolutely certain that veterinary science is the career path that I wish to follow.

I was awarded a prestigious Army 6th Form Scholarship in 2005, securing a place at Sandhurst upon the completion of my studies. I was also the head of the Combined Cadet Force and I regularly return as a Civilian Instructor. Through the CCF I won a Gliding Scholarship from the RAF, achieving my solo wings, and I was invited back to train as an instructor. At school I was a prefect, and also competed in school and house rugby matches. I am a keen rock climber, and have completed two Army training courses, as well as climbing with the school.

I am now studying for two A levels in biology and chemistry in London, and alongside this I am continuing my work at my local vets in Sussex. Over my Christmas break I have also arranged some work experience at the Heathrow Airport Animal Reception Centre, which will show me some of the problems faced when transporting animals around the world, and also introduce me to the vaccines and documents required to do so. As well as this I am going to Wales to help with Christmas lambing, as preparation for the Sussex lambing season.

Notes on personal statement

- Variety of work experience.
- Good examples given.
- Talks about work experience to be done – this can also be a negative as universities require you to have done it already.

However:

- Not enough depth to experiences.
- Too narrative.
- Unclear as to what sparked the move from engineering; on the one hand there is mention of an interest in animals from a young age and on the other it was feeling suffocated by others.
- In some ways too much gap filling, which is evident as there is not too much work experience to rely on.

Example personal statement 5 (3,806 characters with spaces)

Growing up in high-rise concrete-jungle Singapore places limits on exposure to wildlife and common animals. I was fortunate to have lived in an English colonial house with a large backyard, where we housed a dog, three rabbits and a flock of chickens. Early exposure to household pets cultivated my interest in working with animals. Learning about wildlife conservation, microbiology and conservation efforts by Diane Fossey and Jane Goodall has greatly influenced me to work in the veterinary medical field.

To gain an insight into the welfare of domestic animals in Singapore, I joined the Society for the Prevention of Cruelty to Animals (SPCA) in 2011 as a shelter helper and ambassador to promote adoption of homeless pets. I assisted the animal officers in giving out medication, and observed them doing emergency treatments. The large number of injured or homeless pets coming into the shelter and being put to sleep due to the lack of space to accommodate them highlighted the lack of welfare and protection laws for strays. Volunteering at the SPCA has greatly motivated me to become a vet and thus have the knowledge and experience to improve animal welfare and the laws that protect animals in Singapore. I also worked as a veterinary assistant for three months in Singapore. I witnessed dental treatments, castrations and small tumour removals and learnt how to carry out nebulisation processes and perform X-rays on small animals. Witnessing euthanasia and understanding the need for it prepared me to face unexpected situations and to have a pragmatic outlook when dealing with such cases. To see the vets working around the clock showed me the amount of commitment and motivation required to work in the medical field, and the need to constantly learn and improve my knowledge. I learnt how to speak objectively and clearly and to be calm and prepared when handling panic-stricken owners by observing the way the vets communicated with them.

This summer I worked at the Ginny Day Care Centre, where dogs were sent for training and day care. There, I learnt how to manage dogs with behavioural issues such as anxiety. Working with the trainers taught me how to be innovative in my problem-solving skills, as well as to be always on the ball and be prepared to face different reactions from the dogs. To further improve my communication skills I worked at a local cafe in Singapore, which gave me a different perspective on customers when working behind the counter. I have learnt to be patient in understanding the needs of an individual. Since arriving in the UK I have begun to volunteer at the Vauxhall City Farm on a weekly basis to learn more about farming processes as well as gain experience working with large animals.

I have been an athlete throughout my school life, representing my secondary school and junior college in the 100m and 200m at the National Inter-School Track and Field competitions in Singapore. Rigorous training sessions over the years have taught me discipline and perseverance. I am an avid reader of fiction, astronomy and paleontology and I maintain an environment and nature blog, where I post pictures and excerpts from nature articles and professional wildlife photographers. I believe that the UK would be a perfect place to study as it would give me the opportunity to work with and experience small domestic pets, livestock as well as exotics. Following British veterinary students' blogs was a great eye-opener as it showed me life at UK veterinary schools and the different cases they got to work with.

The meeting point between ethics and science encompasses the study and practice of veterinary medicine. With my enthusiasm and persevering nature, I believe that I will be able to contribute to the continual progress of the veterinary medical industry.

Notes on personal statement

- Interesting contextualisation.
- Range of work experience.
- Analysed skills gained on work experience.
- Genuinely interesting personal statement.

However:

- A bit narrative.
- Lists a blog they have written but does not provide a link.
- No link to current studies.

Example personal statement 6 (3,991 characters with spaces)

I grew up surrounded by ducks and chickens and breeding poultry for three years with the use of an incubator gave me an early introduction to veterinary science. This experience allowed me to follow the lifecycle of these birds, tracking their embryonic physiology and growth through the use of candling the eggs, which fascinated me. My choice of A Level subjects helped develop my analytical skills, allowing me to engage in debates and strengthen my reasoning ability. Studying biology gave me an insight into the anatomy and pathogens of animals, as well as the biotechnological processes required to manufacture medicines and genetically manipulate genes and cells for transplant. Chemistry has made me more aware of the fundamental molecules that make up organisms and our environment.

My work experience has further motivated me, and my three weeks' experience at a small-animal practice enabled me to shadow a vet's daily routines as well as observing the work involved both in the operating theatre and in dealing directly with animals and their owners. This gave me an insight into the qualities required by a veterinary surgeon, who must show patience and precision in surgery, as well as compassion and communication skills during consults. My week at Seers Croft Practice was of particular interest as working in their specialist unit enabled me to see reptiles being treated. A particular highlight was monitoring a tortoise recovering from a spay operation; the care and expertise involved in dealing with such a specialised animal was instructive and rewarding.

A week on a farm allowed me to gain hands-on experience delivering lambs and I also had to deal with common ailments associated with lambing, such as newborn lambs who are easily susceptible to infection, to a prolapse of a ewe. My week on a dairy farm was particularly valuable as it allowed me to see the difference between small-animal veterinary medicine compared to a farm, where I assisted in routine procedures such as identifying White Line Disease in cow hooves, dressing wounds and blisters, learning the prevention and cure of mastitis and caring for calves. I was fortunate to witness a surgical procedure of a LDA on a heifer, allowing me to appreciate the physical strength and determination required by the vet. In comparison, working at a professional showing yard for horses allowed me to appreciate the level of management through balancing correct nutrition with the exercise required to produce an animal for the show ring, while ensuring the prevention of laminitis which has been on the increase in 2014. By subscribing to www.vetsonline.com and reading the *Veterinary Times* I have become aware of recent issues and news in veterinary medicine.

Through my varied work experience I have been able to appreciate the responsibility given to veterinary surgeons and others working with animals. As well as being given a degree of responsibility on my work experience, helping out at my local Pony Club camp for the past three years meant that I supervised the safety of 30 riders and their ponies and this also strengthened my communication skills by interacting with the children and their parents. Walking rescue dogs for three months as a part of my Duke of Edinburgh award allowed me to be responsible for dogs who had been ill-treated and taught me the importance of team work. My hobbies include being a member of the school hockey team, a chamber choir, gaining Grade 8 in Singing and captaining the riding team for my college at the National School Equestrian Championships. Overall, my achievements in horse riding and music required me to have patience, determination and commitment, which I believe will be invaluable qualities in veterinary medicine.

I fully appreciate the responsibility, challenges and rewards associated with veterinary medicine and I believe that my academic ability, enthusiasm, determination and passion for animals will allow me to excel in this profession.

Notes on personal statement

- Interesting start.
- Range of work experience.
- Analysed skills gained on work experience.
- Good structure.

However:

- A bit vague in places, such as *Veterinary Times*; would be better to use examples.
- Paragraph on extracurricular activities is a bit long; reads like a CV.

A 'perfect personal statement' is one that you are happy with. It is easier to say what makes a 'bad' personal statement than a 'perfect' one as the latter is such a subjective word. For example, there are always good points and bad points to a personal statement, as highlighted above, and some of these were actually part of successful applications, and yet we are still able to pick out points to discuss. You should just bear in mind that it needs to be an accurate reflection of you.

Bear in mind also that the clever personal statements will look at the course requirements, which are roughly the same for different universities (see pages 48–50), and discuss them in the personal statement.

General tips

- Do not copy anyone else's personal statement. There is no point as it will not reflect you. At the end of the day, you will only ever go wrong if you are not true to yourself. The clue is in the title: it is a 'personal' statement.
- Avoid quotes; these are your words, remember.
- Make sure you proofread your personal statement to check for careless errors; these may be easier to spot if you print off a copy before sending it off.
- Before submitting your application, ask someone else (for example, one of your teachers or a careers adviser) to check the statement for errors.
- However, do not get too many people to read it as, ultimately, everyone will have a different opinion as a personal statement is an individual reaction. It needs to be what you are happy with.
- Keep a copy of your personal statement so you can remind yourself of what you wrote, should you be invited to interview, and make sure you are happy and able to discuss all aspects of your statement, as this will form the basis of the interview.

- The best type of personal statement is one that interprets the experiences and relates them back to your learning.
- Unique experiences are ones that have developed you as a person and helped to confirm this course decision.

Advice from the admissions tutors:

'Really think why you wish to do this course. Too often people say the same thing over and over, which makes it hard to believe – i.e. don't say you have wanted to do this all your life, for that very reason! If that is in fact true, what is more interesting is why you have wanted to do this for such a long time.'

'Please be very careful when footnoting anything that is shown on TV. It is not strictly accurate, and is often designed to make good viewing for the audience as opposed to showing the more routine elements of being a vet which are incredibly important. If you are going to mention something, make sure it is for a purpose.'

'Referencing back to what you are learning at A level and how your knowledge has been useful in understanding the work you did is a very good way of writing your personal statement and one students often miss.'

'Work experience is only useful to write down if you can explain what you learnt doing it, otherwise there is nothing we can take from it other than a list. We do put a good deal of emphasis onto work experience, so please be detailed as we have to compare personal statements against each other. It will also form the basis of some questions at interview.'

Fact: Horses use facial expressions to communicate with each other.

7 | So why did the chicken cross the road?
The interview

When the veterinary schools have received the UCAS applications, they will sift through them and decide who to call for interview. Only approximately one in three applicants to each institution will get an interview, but this can vary from year to year and between universities.

Don't be afraid of the big, bad interviewer. They will huff and puff, but if you make your house out of bricks you will remain firm and resolute in your interview.

Timing

The timing of interviews can be anything from November to March, so some candidates have to wait some time before getting their interview, and because of this timescale some candidates will get a late decision. The Cambridge colleges usually conduct their interviews in December, along with those for other courses at the university.

The purpose of the interview

The interview is designed to find out more about you. In particular, the interviewers (possibly a panel) will want to satisfy themselves about your motivation and the extent of your commitment to becoming a qualified veterinary surgeon, and so they may ask you about the following areas.

- Have you an appropriate attitude towards animal welfare?
- Are you reasonably well informed about the implications of embarking on a veterinary career?
- Are you a mature person possessing a balanced outlook on life?
- Will they be satisfied that you have the ability to cope with the pace of what is generally acknowledged to be a long and demanding course?

To help them they will have your UCAS application, your referee's report and any supporting statements made by veterinary practitioners or people for whom you have worked. They will already have a good idea of your academic ability.

MMIs

An increasingly common type of interview is the Multiple Mini Interview (MMI) format. These consist of different stations, each designed to test students and their abilities in varying stages, considering everything from academic to communicative skills to logic and reason. The key is to always remember that there are not always right and wrong answers, only answers that require more logic and thought. You must therefore be prepared to balance answers and utilise intuition over prior knowledge.

If you will be having an MMI then it would be a good idea to ask multiple members of staff at your school to ask you different questions and get you to think on your feet.

Example of an MMI

We asked for the experiences of different students in their MMIs and their feedback was as follows:

Constructing a triangle

'The data sheet said to choose a correct length wire, bend it from 1.5cm at 60 degrees and the rest of the wire every 4cm with again 60 degrees to form the triangle shown, which was an isosceles triangle with 1.5cm missing at one line of the triangle.'

Drug calculation

'They gave me the rates on how many moles of a specific drug should be used for a certain kilo of a dog. They then told me the weight of another dog and told me to calculate how much that one had to receive. They then gave how much mg/mole of that drug would be, so I had to calculate how many mg it would take to inject that dog. Then they said, under a certain condition, 40% less should be given to the dog and asked me to calculate how much he should then receive.'

Scenario-based

'They asked me what would I do if I was a veterinarian and someone's cat died and they were really sad; so I had to role play this in order to tell them that their cat just died. They wanted to know how I would tell them the news. I talked about having empathy but not sympathy because I need to be able to see how they would feel but that I could not let myself feel as this might affect my performance with the rest of the animals.'

Scenario-based

'They asked me what would I do if one day I was walking with my dog in a forest near a road (and I wasn't using a leash) and all of a sudden he ran off somewhere and started barking. When I approached I saw that he was barking at a badger and I noticed that the badger wasn't able to move but I didn't know why.

'I talked about what the different factors were which might have caused the badger to become immobile and I said I would look to see if there were any shots on him as this might mean a farmer might have tried to kill him due to bovine TB; we then talked about the current issue of badger culling and that even though there was culling, it is now considered to be acceptable if it is done in a humane way in a cage. This wasn't the case, so I said I would make sure to let the police or the RSPCA (Royal Society for Prevention of Cruelty to Animals) know about the situation. I also said I would take my dog away immediately to protect him from TB. I knew that even though the question wasn't asking for it, they wanted a link with bovine TB and badgers.'

Data handing

'There was a table comparing three different things about pigs (their weight, how much they eat and how much money was spent on food) in three different farms (Farm A: normal farm, Farm B: top 30, Farm C: top 5). I had to then describe the graph. They then asked me which farm I thought was the best and why. Then they asked me how could Farm A improve (they were giving so much food to animals so they were spending too much money on food) and I said get food with higher nutrients instead so that less amount could still have enough energy.'

Panel

'They were mostly asking me about my experiences. They then asked about my riding, why I wanted to study in their university, how living abroad helped me and how it made me realise the different aspects, what I learned at my work experiences and about the experiential moments I had.

'One thing I noticed was that they would ask a question about one thing and then change the subject and ask about something else and then go back to the first question they asked and ask further questions about it. It felt like they were trying to see if I could keep up with the fast changes and also to see if I was telling them the truth. They also kept checking my hands and legs to see if they were shaking or not. Most of the questions they asked were related to me and it felt like they were trying to see if I was actually excited to become a veterinarian. If I got one thing out of these experiences, it would be that they want to see your passion and also they want you to make links with everything without them having to tell you to do so.'

Preparation

Experience shows that personal qualities are just as important as academic ability, perhaps more so. The way you come across will be influenced by how confident you are. This does not mean being over-confident. Many people believe that they can get through interviews by thinking on their feet and taking each question as it comes. This is probably an unwise attitude. Good preparation is the key. By being well informed on a variety of issues you will be able to formulate answers to most questions. There will always be the unexpected question for which no amount of preparation can help, but you can minimise the chance of this happening.

Confidence based on good preparation is the best kind. It is not the puffed-up variety that can soon be punctured by searching questions. While it is true that the interviewers will want to put you at your ease and will try to make the atmosphere informal and friendly, there is no doubt that for you there will be some tension in the situation. Think positively – this may be no bad thing. Many of us perform better when we are on our toes.

Some schools will be able to offer you a mock interview. Sometimes they can arrange for a person from outside the school to give the interview, which can help make it feel more realistic. If you are not sure about whether this facility is available, ask your school careers department. They will be keen to help if they can.

If you know anyone, student or staff, connected with one of the veterinary schools, ask for their advice. They may be able to give you an idea of what to expect. Start your preparation by looking at your copy of the personal statement you submitted to UCAS. This is the most important part of your UCAS application and it should tell the interviewers a lot about you as a person, your work experience, your interests and skills. Many of the questions they ask will be prompted by what you have written in it. The questions will most likely begin with those designed to put you at your ease. As the interview proceeds you should expect them to become more searching. Try practising your answers to questions such as those shown below.

Question: *Did you have any trouble getting here?*

Comment: This is the sort of friendly question that is meant to get you started. Do not spend too long on it, but take the opportunity to be sociable, try to relax – and smile.

Question: *Have you visited here before?*

Comment: Did you go to the open day? If so, this is the moment to mention the fact. The interviewer will almost certainly follow up and ask what you thought of it. The faculty probably invested a lot of time and work in preparing it, so go easy on criticism! However, you should be prepared to say what you found was helpful and informative. It is then easier to make an additional constructive criticism. Bear in mind that the interviewers will expect you to have done your homework. If you hope to spend the next five or six years of your life at that institution, you should certainly have made efforts to see whether it is the right place for you. Although your choice is limited to four out of eight veterinary schools, you still have a choice to make. If you answer, 'No, but I've heard that you have a good reputation,' you are hardly likely to convince them that you really want to go there. Similarly, answering, 'No, but I think that all of the veterinary schools are pretty similar' will not enhance your chances.

Question: *What did you think of our brochure?*

Comment: This is an alternative opening question on which you may have an opinion. Some veterinary schools, such as London, have their own brochure; others have entries in the main prospectus. Be prepared: show that you have at least read it and have an opinion. You could say: 'I thought that it was very informative about the structure of the course, and I particularly liked the case histories of your students – they made me realise that students in a similar situation to me can get a place.' Hopefully, this will lead to a question which will allow you to talk about your experience.

Question: *How do you think you are doing with your A levels?*

Comment: This is not a time for modesty. You would not be having this interview if your school had not predicted that you will get good results. You should be sounding optimistic while at the same time indicating that you are working hard. They may also be interested to learn what your favourite subjects are, so be ready for a follow-up question along those lines. You could talk about a biology project that was relevant to veterinary science. As with the two previous examples, your aim should be to steer these rather boring questions towards topics that you have prepared and that will show you in the strongest light.

Question: *What do you think of the TV programmes about vets?*

Comment: Nowadays, programmes specifically about vets in the UK are seen as less marketable than programmes such as those documenting wildlife abroad or those featuring celebrities such as Sir David Attenborough: human nature is such that people are more interested by the exotic or the unknown. A few years ago there were several programmes on television following the everyday work of a vet. Such programmes were not always good for the professional standing of the vet. They made entertaining television, especially when they showed the animals and the caring 'honest broker' role of the vet between animals and humankind. They also almost universally presented vets as amiable people. On the other hand, though, you could argue that veterinary science was undermined when the programmes degenerated into 'soaps', with a portrayal of young vets whose work was an easy or incidental part of their lives. In your answer, show that you have thought about television's influence.

Question: *Why do you want to study veterinary science?*

Comment: The direction of the interview can change quite suddenly. Be ready for the switch in questioning; the answer will bring into focus your attitude to animals, the range of your work experience, those important manual skills, and your commitment to all the hard work entailed in studying to become a qualified professional veterinary surgeon admitted to the register of the RCVS. This is your opportunity, if you have not already done so, to mention your work experience, and to emphasise how your determination to become a vet increased as a result. This is an important question and needs a full answer, but keep your reply to less than two minutes. Practise this. Remember that research findings show that if you exceed two minutes you risk boring your listeners.

Question: *Why do you want to come to this veterinary school?*

Comment: This is a natural follow-up question, so be prepared for it. The answer is personal to you: you may want to go to a new area of the country; you may know the area well because you have relations living there; your local vet may have recommended this particular veterinary school to you; the reputation of the school may have impressed you because of some particular specialty in which you are also interested. There could be several reasons, but make sure you give an honest answer, not just what you think the interviewer wants to hear.

Question: *Tell us something about your work experience with animals.*

Comment: This is one of the big questions of the interview. It would be surprising if the interviewers do not already have feedback from where you have been working. The interviewers will know what happens in a veterinary practice or on a farm, so lists of things that you saw or did will not shed any light on your suitability for the profession. Instead, concentrate on your reactions to the experience. Did you enjoy it? Were there any interesting or unusual cases that stick in your memory? Is your enthusiasm clear? Do you show your respect and sympathy for the animals? And what about the people – did you get on with them? The key phrases here are 'For example, when I …' and 'For instance, I was able to …'.

Question: *What are the main things you learned from your work experience?*

Comment: This is the typical follow-up question that gives you a chance to summarise and underline your impressions. You could try to indicate the varied nature of your experience and the different types of practice or farms you saw. There is also the business side of working with animals, for which you may not originally have been prepared. Maybe you were astonished at the responsibilities of the veterinary nurses. Be prepared to intrigue your listeners. A related question is: 'From your work experience, what do you think are the qualities necessary to be a successful vet?' Rather than answering 'Stamina, communication, physical fitness, problem solving …' and so on, bring in examples of things that you saw. For example: 'The ability to solve problems. For instance, when I accompanied a vet to a riding school, it was clear that one of the horses was very distressed, but it was unclear why …' and then go on to explain the steps involved in the diagnosis and treatment.

Question: *Have you ever felt frightened of animals?*

Comment: Vets shouldn't be frightened of animals, particularly small ones! However, honesty compels most of us to admit that we have at times and in certain situations felt vulnerable to a kick or bite. Explain the situation and what was said at the time – vets are noted for their humour!

Question: *What do you think of rearing animals for meat?*

Comment: This type of question might be asked because it checks on your motivation. Perhaps you should start by looking at it from the animal's viewpoint. Animals should be kept well, with good standards of husbandry, and eventually slaughtered humanely. Of course, the animal does not know the reason for its slaughter, but you do. Some of your future clients may be farmers who make their living from supplying meat or poultry – what is your reaction? If you oppose eating meat, you should be honest but make it clear that you would be able to remain professional.

Question: *How do you feel about cruelty to animals?*

Comment: With the strong interest in and liking for animals that you would expect from all veterinary students, they will be watching your reaction. This is a question that you should expect and your response, while putting animal welfare first, should be strong and well reasoned rather than too emotional. What would you do if you thought a farmer was acting in a cruel way to some of his livestock? Go to the police straight away? Talk over the difficulty with a colleague? Threaten the farmer by mentioning that you might bring in the RSPCA? The interviewers are not expecting you to come up with a perfect answer but rather to show that you are capable of coming up with a well-balanced and reasoned solution.

Question: *What are your views on euthanasia?*

Comment: They are looking for your ability to balance an argument. Any relevant examples would be helpful. Talk about it from the point of view of the animal and the owner. Do not be concerned about your own feelings as this is the job you wish to do and this is a regrettable part of it. Think of it from a humane point of view versus a human response. Also consider the implications of putting a horse down at the races (the Grand National for example) as there are obviously financial issues at play as well.

Question: *How important is the business element of veterinary medicine?*

Comment: Remember, some vets have to be business people as well. Smaller practices rely on the vets themselves to manage the practice. Therefore, you must be prepared to be strong when asking people for money, even in the face of tragedy for them. That can be hard, but the practice's survival is mostly based on your ability to recoup your charges.

There will, of course, be questions on your scientific knowledge and current topics (listed on page 102). Be prepared to answer many different types of questions, such as:

- What injections does a kitten require?
- Why haven't you got specific work experience in a particular area?
- Is training to help animals a good use of public money?
- If you have been to an abattoir (specifically for Liverpool), how do you slaughter an animal?

The Student Room (www.thestudentroom.co.uk) is often a very good place to visit as students exchange their experiences and questions at interview. There are some great questions on there, such as, 'How lambs obtained immunity from their mothers and how that differed from humans'. It is very important to take what is written with a pinch of salt, though, as it is a subjective forum and one person's experience is not the same as another's. You will see stories of tough and unfriendly interview panels in the same discussion thread as someone else who found them to be very friendly.

The message really is do not believe every horror story that is written. More often than not, an interview panel is there to simply find out what you know and not to test you beyond your limits. Sometimes you will get questions that you do not know the answer to and in those situations you should feel confident in asking them to explain further and saying that you do not know, instead of trying to make the answer up. You can then have an informed discussion instead of them forming a view about you.

Remember: Good preparation is key.

Case study

Grace has just finished the third year of her veterinary course at the University of Bristol. She is 21 years old and is looking forward to beginning the fourth and fifth years of her training.

'I grew up in rural South Wales with lots of pets and always knew that I wanted to become a vet. I didn't take my GCSEs as seriously as I should have done but managed to get decent grades and really began to work hard when I entered my A levels. After receiving top grades in biology, chemistry and mathematics, along with a strong BMAT score, I was offered places at both Bristol and Liverpool.

'I know everyone says the same thing, but what I learned from the process of applying for veterinary courses was the importance of work experience. After my GCSEs, I visited the careers advisor at my school who told me that these placements would be vital for my university application. I found it difficult to secure places at first, but after spending some time shadowing my family vet, she put me in contact with other practices in my local area. I was also fortunate to live near a big working farm and they allowed me to help out each year during lambing season.

'I always knew that I wanted to be close to home for university so the University of Bristol was the obvious choice. Although the first three years have been really hard work, I am really enjoying it and it has only reinforced to me that this is the career I want to pursue. I know the fourth year will be a challenge but I am looking forward to beginning my studies this year at the Langford campus.

'After speaking to others on my course, I know that I was lucky in my application and it isn't such a smooth process for everyone. I think the key is to prepare yourself and to take all opportunities that may help to give you a better knowledge of what it is to be a vet. It was great that in my university interviews I could answer confidently about the work experience that I had done and I think this showed how passionate I am about following this career path.'

Topical and controversial issues

Your interviewer will want to find out whether you are genuinely interested in the profession, and alongside work experience, this includes testing your knowledge, awareness and appreciation of important issues: after all, if you are planning to devote the next 40 or so years of your life to veterinary science, you ought to be interested in issues that affect the profession. It could be about the diseases currently affecting the profession or the latest idea of dog pre-nups to safeguard the animal in situations of broken homes.

Most interviews last only 15 to 20 minutes, so there may not be time for questions of a more topical or controversial nature. Nevertheless, it may be worth investing a little thought into how you might sketch out an answer to questions covering one or more of the following issues, each of which will be outlined in this chapter:

- Ebola
- avian influenza (bird flu)
- bovine tuberculosis (TB) and badgers
- bluetongue disease
- canine influenza
- methicillin-resistant *Staphylococcus aureus* (MRSA)
- foot-and-mouth disease
- bovine spongiform encephalopathy (BSE)
- animal obesity
- canine lungworm
- Schmallenberg virus
- swine influenza virus
- anthrax
- Aujeszky's disease
- intensive farming
- fox hunting
- fall of dairy prices
- High Profile Breed List for dogs
- Dangerous Dogs Act
- hybrid dogs
- animal testing.

This is not an exhaustive list but deals with the most current and topical issues in the veterinary profession. It would be worthwhile visiting www.gov.uk and www.dardni.gov.uk for a complete list of issues affect-ing animals in the UK.

Remember, most of the time there is no right or wrong answer for questions relating to issues such as these. It is really a case of demon-strating your understanding of an issue, your quality of judgement and your ability to discuss the issue clearly, logically and succinctly. A burst of enthusiasm and conviction won't do any harm either.

It goes without saying that the more informed you are, the more realistic your chance of entering this profession, so keeping up to date with recent developments affecting the veterinary profession is not only important but compulsory. The best sources of information are the broadsheet newspapers and internet news websites such as that of the British Veterinary Association (BVA: www.bva.co.uk). As well as the news sections, the health sections contain articles that will be of interest.

Read a newspaper every day, cut out or photocopy articles of interest, and keep them in a scrapbook so that you can revise from them before your interview. You will also find the Defra website (www.defra.gov.uk) extremely helpful. Other useful websites are listed in Chapter 12.

Questions on these issues are your chance to display a depth of knowl-edge from which you can open a discussion and show the clarity of analytical thought needed to be a vet. In many ways it is symptomatic of the profession and therefore good preparation. Good research ahead of your interview will also give you the confidence to feel able to discuss these issues with a professional.

At the time of going to print, the issues below are the most important current topics affecting the industry within recent years.

Ebola

The Ebola virus disease or EVD (previously Ebola haemorrhagic fever) is an often fatal illness in humans. While not a strict veterinary issue, it is useful to understand how it originated. The virus is contracted from wild animals and is spread through human transmission. At present, the fatality rate is about 39.5%, according to the World Health Organization (WHO), but in the past that has reached 90%. The WHO declared West Africa in January 2016 to now be Ebola-free. However, they have advised that other flare ups may occur in the future and that the disease has not been erased completely. It is suspected that animals such as fruit bats are Ebola virus hosts and they spread it through the animal kingdom, passing it on to other animals. In turn, humans contract the virus when they come into contact with blood or other secretions from animals such as chimpanzees, monkeys, gorillas or forest antelope to name but a few. The WHO recommends that greater care should be taken when handling animals in that area, ensuring gloves and appropriate clothing are worn when handling any animal. Equally, meat should be well cooked. Defra is also in the process of recommending a cull of guinea pigs in order to stop the spread of Ebola.

Avian influenza (bird flu)

The first human case of avian influenza or bird flu was in Hong Kong in 1997. Before then it wasn't known that this type of illness could be passed from birds directly to humans. The virus is spread when infected birds excrete the virus in their faeces. Once this dries it becomes a powder and is therefore easily inhaled. Symptoms are similar to other types of flu – fever, malaise, sore throat and coughing. People can also develop conjunctivitis. All 18 people infected in 1997 had been in close contact with live birds in markets or on farms.

Countries known to have been affected by the disease include Cambodia, Indonesia, South Korea, China, Japan, Thailand, Vietnam and Hong Kong. Furthermore, since January 2004, human cases of avian influenza have been reported in Asia, Africa, the Pacific region and Europe. Avian flu has been seen to have a high fatality rate in humans. In 1997, six out of the 18 people who were infected died. In an outbreak in 2004, there were over 20 confirmed deaths.

There are 15 different strains of the virus, but it is the H5N1 strain that infects humans and causes high death rates. Even within the H5N1 strain, however, variations are seen, and slightly different strains are being seen in the different countries where there have been outbreaks of the disease. The H5N1 virus that emerged in Asia in 2003 continues to evolve and may adapt so that other mammals may be susceptible to infection as well. Moreover, it is likely that H5N1 infection among birds has become endemic in certain areas and that human infections resulting from direct contact with infected poultry and/or wild birds will continue to occur. So far, the spread of the H5N1 virus from person to person has been rare and limited.

Patients suffering from avian flu are treated often with antiviral drugs while researchers continue to work to develop a vaccine, though the difficulty is it develops into new strains over time. In 2004, the EU announced that it was considering a precautionary ban on the importation of poultry meat and products from Thailand. At the same time, millions of birds were culled in an attempt to stop the spread of the disease among birds, which would in turn prevent it being passed on to humans. Currently, there is a ban on the importation of birds and bird products from H5N1-affected countries. The regulation states that no person may import or attempt to import any birds, whether dead or alive, or any products derived from birds (including hatching eggs), from the specified countries.

In January 2006, two children from the eastern Turkish town of Dogubeyazit, whose family kept poultry at their home, died having contracted the virulent H5N1 strain. Three months later, in the Scottish town of Fife, tests confirmed that a swan there had died from the deadly H5N1 strain of the avian flu virus. The discovery made Britain the four-teenth country in Europe to have the disease in its territory. The first major outbreak in the UK was in February 2007, on a turkey farm in Suffolk. In November 2008, the UK became free from avian influenza as defined by the rules of the World Organisation for Animal Health (OIE). As of October 2014, the WHO confirmed that, globally, avian influenza had a confirmed 667 human cases, which led to 393 deaths, between 2003 and 2014. The AHVLA (Animal Health and Veterinary Laboratories Agency) conducts checks every year to determine whether avian influenza is present and publishes guidelines on www.gov.uk on how to spot it in birds. A strain of bird flu (H5N8) was found at a duck breeding farm in Yorkshire in 2014, though Defra ruled it low risk for public health. More recently, bird flu was confirmed in poultry in Hampshire in February 2015, though it was a lesser strain H7N7. Twenty-one days after infection, controls were lifted as the disease was contained and cleared. The last reported case of the more deadly N5N1 was in the first part of 2008.

In 2016, a case of avian influenza was confirmed in Scotland in January of that year on a poultry farm. Restrictions were put in place around the farm, and were lifted in February after tests confirmed the disease to no longer be of concern at that time.

Bovine tuberculosis and badgers

Bovine tuberculosis (bTB) is a serious disease in cattle. Although the risk of tuberculosis spreading to humans through milk or meat is slight, it can be transmitted through other means, particularly to farm workers who have direct contact with the animals. The number of cattle slaughtered because of bTB has increased from 599 in 1986 to 39,728 for the year ending September 2016 across England and Wales.

There is uncertainty about the cause of the spread of bTB in cattle, but many people believe that it is passed on by badgers – a protected species. There is widespread support within the farming community for the culling of badgers, but this is opposed by wildlife and conservation groups. Nearly 20 years ago, in 1998, the government set up a badger-culling trial as well as taking steps to test the carcasses of badgers killed on the roads (about 50,000 every year) in order to try to find out more about the causes of the disease in cattle. However, the results were inconclusive, and the two opposing sides in the argument are still at loggerheads: the fundamental question remains unanswered – is bTB spread from badgers to cattle, from cattle to badgers, or is other wildlife involved?

Then, in November 2004, the government introduced enhanced testing and control measures to help improve the detection of bTB, so that action could be taken quickly to prevent the spread of the disease. A 10-year government strategic framework for the sustainable control of bTB in Great Britain was later published in March 2005. Through this framework, the government aimed to bring about a sustainable improvement in control of bTB by 2015. In December 2005, the government also announced pre-movement testing in England and Wales to help reduce the risk of bTB spreading between herds.

According to data, there was a reduction in the number of new bTB incidents in 2005 and again in 2006. Despite that reduction, however, levels of bTB remained high in comparison with other EU countries. On 7 July 2008, Hilary Benn MP, the then Secretary of State for Environment, Food and Rural Affairs, issued a statement to Parliament about bTB and badgers which declared that government policy was that licences would not be issued to allow badger culling to control bTB for fear that the cull might make things worse. He went on to say that £20 million would be invested in vaccinations for badgers and cattle over three years. Mr Benn also intimated that he wanted to work closely with the farming industry in order to find the appropriate solution and, in conjunction with Defra, a Bovine TB Partnership Group was to be established. After the success of its work, in 2012, Jim Paice, the Agriculture Minister, announced a new Bovine TB Eradication Advisory Group for England which was to broaden into areas of conservation.

In this period, bTB was at its most prevalent. While Defra statistics showed a notable decrease in the incidence rate in 2012 in cattle, to 4.2%, compared with 6.0% in June 2011 (mainly as a result of an increased number of tests on unrestricted herds), cattle were, and are, still slaughtered in large numbers. Defra, however, advises that this figure of 4.2% should not be accepted as 100% accurate, as it included a number of unclassified incidents and there were further revisions made. Herd incidents during the period January to June 2012 were 2,706, compared with 2,720 for January to June 2011. The number of tests on officially bTB-free herds was 41,656 in January to June 2012, compared with 34,667 in January to June 2011. The number of cattle compulsorily slaughtered as reactors or direct contacts was 18,213 in January to June 2012, compared with 18,081 in January to June 2011.

That said, the debate continues as there is huge resistance to the culling of badgers; opponents say that it risks increasing the spread of bTB instead of decreasing it. Leading experts on animal diseases say that, even if the increase does not materialise, culling is very unlikely to eradicate the spread of bTB, and they are angered over government plans that suggest a cull of 70% of badgers in an area will stop the spread of bTB. Many high-profile figures have joined the opposition at various stages, with Queen guitarist Brian May publicly lending his support, and several petitions to stop the cull have been signed and sent to Parliament.

In the past few years the picture has moved on. From 2013, badger culls were undertaken to try to control the spread of this disease in pilot areas in west Somerset and west Gloucestershire. The secretary of state confirmed in 2014 that these licences would continue in the pilot areas; however, before the culls were to be rolled out in other areas, the process would be improved following a review into the humaneness of the operation. In June 2014, the number of new herd incidents was 2,398 compared to 2,535 in the equivalent period in 2013, with 17,063 cattle slaughtered.

In the most recent update review in 2014, the government said it had achieved some degree of success with the policy mentioned above, laid out in 2005, and revised their target to become Officially Bovine Tuberculosis Free to 2038, within an interim objective of 'likely to be' in 2025 for large parts of the north and east of England.

However, in 2016, there was growing concern as bTB cases were on the rise, particularly in Cornwall. This continues to be one of the biggest animal health concerns in Great Britain and there is a growing political clamour for more widespread badger culls to control the spread of the problem, even though new research shows that contact with badgers is not necessary in the spread of the disease. The last figures for the extent of the problem revealed that 36,000 cattle were slaughtered at a cost of £100 million to the taxpayer.

Bluetongue disease

Bluetongue, which has now been downgraded by Defra in its level of severity, is an insect-borne viral disease to which all species of ruminants are susceptible, although sheep are most severely affected. It is characterised by changes to the mucous linings of the mouth and nose and the coronary band of the foot. It was first described in South Africa but has since been recognised in most countries in the tropics and subtropics. Since 1999, there have been widespread outbreaks in Greece, Italy, Corsica and the Balearic Islands. Cases have also occurred in Bulgaria, Croatia, Macedonia and Serbia. It appears that the virus has spread from both Turkey and north Africa. One possible reason for the changing pattern of bluetongue disease in the Mediterranean region is climate changes. In September 2007, the first suspected UK case was reported in a Highland cow in Ipswich, Suffolk. Since then the virus has spread from cattle to sheep in Britain.

The clinical signs can vary from unapparent to mild or severe, depending on the virus strain and the breed of sheep involved. Deaths of sheep in a flock can be as high as 70%. Animals that survive the disease will lose condition, with a reduction in meat and wool production.

Bluetongue has been found in Australia, the USA, Africa, the Middle East and other parts of Asia and in Europe – with cases reported in the Netherlands, Belgium, parts of western Germany and areas of northern France. In order to control the infection, a protection zone boundary of 20km is set up to control the movement of animals and a further surveillance zone of 150km is put in place to monitor for any signs of the disease spreading. In the restriction zone, rules apply to the movement of ruminants, export of animals is prohibited and all animals on premises within this zone have to be identified and checked for bluetongue.

After bluetongue serotype 6 (BTV6) was confirmed on three farms in the Netherlands, on 20 October 2008 all exports from the Netherlands to other EU member states were banned as a precautionary measure while these cases were investigated. While there is no ban on exports from Great Britain, there are still bans on imports from certain European zones. There are no reports of transmission to humans. On 5 July 2011, Great Britain was declared bluetongue free. While there are different strains of bluetongue virus, the important strain for Great Britain is known as BTV8.

In October 2014, Glasgow scientists made a breakthrough in adapting bluetongue vaccines to new strains of the disease. This is saving the industry millions, and was introduced nationwide in July 2016, as the BTV8 strain has cost the industry €80 million.

Bluetongue type 8, currently not present in the UK, is currently prevalent around northern France and at the end of summer of 2016, there was an 80% risk of incursion in the UK by being carried by midges and flies from France to south-east England by high winds, according to the National Farmers Union. At the time of writing, the situation is being monitored to see whether that happened and what subsequent cases materialised.

Canine influenza

Canine influenza refers to a new strain of the influenza A virus that causes influenza in canines. It is a contagious respiratory disease that often has the same signs as kennel cough – sneezing, coughing and fever – and requires veterinary medical attention. The disease came to light at a Florida racetrack when greyhound fatalities from respiratory illnesses were attributed to a mutated strain of the deadly equine influenza virus (H3N8) that has been detected in horses for over 40 years. Dogs have no natural immunity to this virus, owing to a lack of previous exposure, and therefore transmission rates between canines are recorded as being very high. Having affected the majority of American states, this specific strain of the influenza virus has now reached endemic levels. Statistically, roughly 100% of canines that come into contact with the virus – regardless of age or vaccination history –

become infected. Of those infected, 20% show no signs of the virus. Of the 80% that exhibit signs, there have been two forms observed:

- mild infection – symptoms include a low fever, possible nasal discharge and a persistent cough that can last for anything up to three weeks
- severe infection – symptoms include a high fever, increased respiratory rates, which lead to difficulty breathing, and potentially other indicators of pneumonia.

However, the more positive news is that research shows fatality in only 8% of infected canines, making it a disease with a high morbidity but a low mortality rate.

Canine influenza is believed to be a mainly airborne virus – i.e. it is transmitted by sneezing or coughing – with an affected dog able to spread the virus for seven to 10 days after contracting the strain. Symptoms will present within two to five days. It is also worth bearing in mind that infected dogs can spread the virus without exhibiting signs of disease in themselves.

Treatment of canine influenza will vary from case to case. Early symptoms may require only a course of antibiotics to stop any secondary bacterial infections, but more serious cases could require the same treatment that humans receive in influenza cases, i.e. fluids (supplied intravenously in severe cases) and rest. There is now a recognised vaccine to control both strains of canine influenza in America and Canada which has just gained approval, with the Bivalent Canine Flu Vaccine being used in the primary stages to prevent contraction of the disease. This is not yet available in the UK. The virus is not known to infect humans or poultry.

MRSA

Methicillin-resistant *Staphylococcus aureus* (MRSA) – or 'superbug' – is a major health concern for causing outbreaks in hospitals around the UK. Primarily affecting humans, as the BVA says, it may also colonise and cause infection in companion and farm animals. MRSA is of little risk to healthy animals and, although transmission of infection from animals to humans has been documented, the rate is thought to be low. The evidence available points to humans as the source of the MRSA strains.

Staphylococcus aureus is a bacterium, strains of which live harmlessly on the skin and in the nose of about a third of normal healthy people. The problem arises when it enters the body, and it thrives in hospitals among those who are more susceptible, due to the nature of their illnesses weakening their immune systems. MRSA can often enter the body through cuts, grazes and wounds, whether accidental or deliberate, i.e. those made out of necessity for surgery.

Different strains of MRSA usually affect animals and humans. They are particularly adept at colonising and/or infecting their preferred host species. For example, the *staphylococci* that commonly infect and colonise dogs are usually from a different species, known as *Staphylococcus intermedius*, which differs in certain characteristics from *Staphylococcus aureus*. Although strains of the latter may have a preferred host species, they can opportunistically infect other species in some circumstances.

Reported cases of MRSA infection in animals can be traced back to 1999 and are often reported in the media, although there was an incident back in the mid-1980s regarding a cat that lived in a rehabilitation ward for the elderly. Since then, dogs, cats, rabbits and horses have all been diagnosed with the MRSA infection. This problem is not isolated to the UK, but is seen throughout the world, with cases reported in the USA, Korea, Japan and Brazil. There is evidence of pigs now being affected in the Netherlands.

Most MRSA infections, particularly in cats and dogs, have been post-operative infections, usually from wounds, though the numbers of skin, ear, urinary tract and bronchial infections have been lower recently. There is evidence of a new strain affecting pigs and poultry but there is still no link with the human strain.

MRSA is a problem that will continue to trouble both humans and animals, because the effectiveness of antibiotics is constantly being challenged by the bacterium developing resistance to the drug.

Foot-and-mouth disease

The outbreak of foot-and-mouth disease (FMD) that occurred in February 2001 was the first in the UK for 20 years. Between February and September, 2,030 cases occurred. The previous major outbreak was in 1967, during which about half a million animals were slaughtered. Before the re-emergence of the disease, in a new and highly virulent form, it had been thought that FMD had been eradicated from western Europe. The latest form of the virus seems to have originated in Asia, and could have been brought into the UK in a number of ways. Something as trivial as a discarded sandwich containing meat from an infected source – brought into the country by, for example, a tourist – could have been incorporated into pigswill (pig feed made from waste food) and then passed on to animals from other farms at a livestock sale. The bovine spongiform encephalopathy (BSE) problem (see pages 112–113) led to greater regulation of abattoirs, which resulted in the closure of many smaller abattoirs. Animals destined for slaughter now have to travel greater distances and the possibility of FMD being passed to other animals is, as a consequence, greater.

The UK was declared FMD-free on 14 January 2002, almost a year after the first reported case. More than 4 million animals, from over

7,000 farms, were slaughtered during this period. The last recorded case occurred at the end of September 2001. The official report into the outbreak highlighted the lack of speed with which the government acted and commented on the fact that the understaffed State Veterinary Service (now called Animal Health) was unable to effectively monitor the disease. The disease took a month to diagnose and, by the time animal movement was halted, over 20,000 infected sheep had spread the virus across the UK.

Defra states that:

> 'FMD is endemic in parts of Asia, Africa and South America, with sporadic outbreaks in disease-free areas. Countries affected by FMD include Afghanistan, Bhutan, Iran, Lebanon, Peru, South Africa, the United Arab Emirates and Vietnam.'
>
> www.defra.gov.uk

There have been no outbreaks of the disease in the EU since the one in 2001, which affected not only the UK but also Ireland, France and the Netherlands. A Royal Society report recommended that vaccination – commonly used in a number of countries – should be a weapon in any future outbreaks. Vaccination is unpopular with some meat exporters since it is difficult to distinguish between animals that have been vaccinated and those that have the disease, and for this reason many FMD-free countries ban the import of vaccinated cattle.

FMD is a viral disease that affects cattle, pigs, sheep, goats and deer. Hedgehogs and rats (and elephants!) can also become infected, and people, cats, dogs and game animals can carry infected material. The virus can be transferred by saliva, milk and dung; it can also become airborne and travel large distances, perhaps as far as 150 miles. A vehicle that has driven through dung from an infected animal can carry the virus to other farms on its tyres. FMD is more contagious than any other animal disease, and the mortality rate among young animals is high.

The role of the veterinary surgeon in a suspected outbreak of FMD is not a pleasant one. If the existence of the disease is confirmed, the vet must make arrangements with Defra to ensure that all animals on the farm (and possibly on neighbouring farms) are slaughtered and then incinerated. For economic reasons, there is no question of the vet being allowed to try to treat infected animals.

There has been only one recorded case of FMD in a human being in Great Britain and that was in 1966. The general effects of the disease in that case were similar to influenza, with some blisters. It is a mild, short-lived, self-limiting disease. The Food Standards Agency has advised that the disease in animals has no implications for the human food chain.

The BVA has warned that 15 years on from the last big outbreak (it is worth noting there was a case in 2007), it is almost impossible to completely rule out the return of foot and mouth to this country. It is at the moment prevalent in Turkey and so there is always a risk, however there are very tight controls in place on the import of animal livestock to this country.

Bovine spongiform encephalopathy (BSE)

BSE – commonly referred to as mad cow disease – was first identified in 1986, although it is possible that it had been known about since 1983. It is a neurological disease that affects the brains of cattle, and is similar to scrapie, a disease of sheep that has been known since the eighteenth century. In 1988, the government's working party, chaired by Sir Richard Southwood, stated that there was minimal risk to humans since, as scrapie was known not to spread to humans, neither would BSE. It is believed that BSE originated in cattle as a result of the practice of using the remains of diseased sheep as part of high-protein cattle feed in an attempt to increase milk yields. In 1989, the government recommended that specific offal – such as the brain and the spleen – should be discarded rather than allowed to enter the food chain, and that diseased cattle should be incinerated. In the early 1990s, the increased incidence of Creutzfeldt–Jakob disease (CJD) – a disease similar to BSE that affects humans – caused scientists to look at the possibility that the disease had jumped species. At about the same time, scientists found increasing evidence of transmission between species following experiments involving mice, pigs and cats. By 1993, there were over 800 new cases of BSE a week, despite the ban on animal feed containing specified offal. It became clear that the increase in the cases of CJD was related to the rise in BSE, and that it was likely that millions of infected cattle had been eaten before the symptoms appeared. In 1996, the EU banned the export of cattle, beef and beef products that originated in the UK. In 1997, the government set up a public inquiry, chaired by Lord Phillips. The findings were released in October 2000 and details can be found on the inquiry website (http://collections.europarchive.org/tna/20090505194948/http:/bseinquiry.gov.uk/report/index.htm). The total number of confirmed cases of BSE in Great Britain since 1986 is estimated to be about 185,000. There has been an overall decline in the epidemic in recent years, with only between one and three cases annually over the last four years.

The BSE problem raised a number of issues concerning farming and food safety. In retrospect, the decision to allow the remains of diseased animals to be incorporated into feed for herbivores seems to have been misguided, at the very least. The problem with BSE is that the infecting agent, the prion (a previously unknown pathogen composed of proteins), was able to survive the treatments used to destroy bacteria and viruses. If any good has come out of the problem, it is that we are now much more aware of food safety. In April 2000, the government established the Food Standards Agency, created to 'protect public health from risks which may arise in connection with the consumption of food, and otherwise to protect the interests of consumers in relation to food'. Although it was established by the government, it can independently publish any advice that it gives the government, in order to avoid the accusations of cover-ups and secrecy levelled at the government over the BSE affair.

In March 2006, EU veterinary experts agreed unanimously to lift the ban on British beef exports, imposed 10 years earlier to prevent the spread of BSE. The EU's standing committee on the food chain and animal health said that the UK had fulfilled all the conditions for the ban to end. The closure of export markets had cost the British beef industry around £675 million.

Animal obesity

Researchers at the University of Glasgow have found that six out of 10 pet dogs are overweight or obese and independent research has shown that one in three household pets are overweight. As with humans, animals are putting on weight as a result of a number of factors, including being fed scraps from the dinner table, lack of exercise and even how old or rich their owners are.

According to the university's website:

> 'The study in the Journal of Small Animal Practice assessed the body condition of 696 dogs. Owners were asked how often they fed their dog, what type of food was given, how often the dog was exercised, and the owner's age and household income. The results showed that 35.3% of the dogs had an ideal body shape, 39% were overweight, and 20.4% were obese; a further 5.3% were underweight.'
>
> Source: www.gla.ac.uk/news/archiveofnews/2010/
> july/headline_164795_en.html

Obesity can have a huge impact on an animal's health as it exacerbates a range of medical conditions, including arthritis and expiratory airway dysfunction, as well as affecting its lifespan.

The income of the owners was a factor:

> 'The dogs whose owners earned less than £10,000 a year were much more likely to be obese or overweight than those whose owners earned £40,000 or more.'
>
> Source: www.gla.ac.uk/news/archiveofnews/
> 2010/july/headline_164795_en.html

This is a problem that has got worse over the past 10 years, and a report from the PFMA (Pet Food Manufacturers Association) highlights that 77% of vets say that obesity has increased since 2009 in birds, cats, dogs and rabbits. This is despite guidelines and incentives being put in place for pet owners. The latest guidelines provide clear instructions for pet owners from portion size to exercise. It comes off the back of a recent study that highlighted that 80% of veterinary professionals had seen an increase in animal weight in the past two years. The pet food industry is big business and it clearly has had an impact on animal health.

Canine lungworm

Angiostrongylus vasorum (or French heartworm) is a parasitic condition that is usually found in canines. Typically found in the heart and major blood vessels, lungworm causes many problems for the dog. If left untreated, it can cause fatal damage. Younger dogs are far more likely to be affected. The parasite is most often carried in slugs and snails and normally ingested by dogs eating these pests. Foxes are also to blame for spreading the disease around the country.

For anyone concerned about this, the signs to look out for are breathing difficulties, poor blood clotting, general sickness and changes in behaviour. While the main concern is obviously for the animal, as untreated it can be fatal, the spread of infection is a major issue. Canine lungworm is spread between canines through larvae in the faeces rather than directly, and so the worry is that dogs will become infected through close contact with the faeces of other dogs. Unlike roundworm, humans cannot become infected with this.

While this particular lungworm is the major cause for concern at the moment, there are also other types that can affect dogs. See www. lungworm.co.uk for more information.

Schmallenberg virus

The Schmallenberg virus is a disease spreading throughout the UK affecting livestock. As the virus spread to the north of England, it was simply a matter of time before it reached Scotland, where it was confirmed in 2013. The virus is thought to be transmitted by infected midges and to have travelled into the UK from the Continent. It is not believed that the outbreak has been brought into the country through imported livestock. The European Centre for Disease Prevention and Control suggests that there is a low risk to public health. It is currently found in Belgium, Germany, the Netherlands and the UK.

Most commonly transmitted by midges, mosquitoes and ticks, it causes mild to moderate disease (milk drop, pyrexia and diarrhoea) in adult cattle and late abortion or birth defects in new-born cattle, sheep and goats.

Lower temperatures reduce the activity of the carriers and therefore the spread of the virus should slow down over the winter.

Reported case numbers are isolated and there are no control measures in place even though the AHVLA is passively observing. There have been no reported cases in 2016. See www.defra.gov.uk/animal-diseases/a-z/schmallenberg-virus for more information.

Swine influenza virus

This is a very common occurrence in pig populations: about half of the USA's pigs are thought to have the virus. While the swine flu outbreak of 2009 made the news in terms of its effects on humans, transmission of the virus from pigs to humans is relatively uncommon and does not always lead to human influenza, often resulting only in the production of antibodies in the blood. While it is uncommon, people with regular exposure to pigs are at increased risk of swine flu infection. If this causes human influenza, it is called zoonotic swine flu.

In pigs, three influenza A virus subtypes (H1N1, H1N2 and H3N2) are the most common strains worldwide. In the United States, the H1N1 subtype was the major strain pre-1998; after this time, H3N2 subtypes have been isolated from swine. As of 2004, H3N2 virus in pigs and turkeys contained human (HA, NA and PB1), swine (NS, NP and M), and avian (PB2 and PA) genes.

Transmission of the influenza virus is between infected and unaffected animals, with close transport, intensive farming and airborne infection all reasons for the spread of infection. Wild boar are considered to spread the disease between farms. The symptoms are sneezing, coughing, lethargy, decreased appetite and difficulty breathing.

As swine influenza is rarely fatal to pigs, little effort is made to treat the infection, with efforts instead being focused on stopping the spread of infection between farms. Antibiotics do exist, though, and are used to treat the symptoms of influenza.

As of 2016, the threat of new strains of flu has increased across different continents, mostly as a result of human flu, which has led to concerns of another future epidemic.

Anthrax

Anthrax is a disease that can survive for centuries as the spores can live on through carcasses, hides and wool. It is then passed on through inhalation, ingestion or through lesions and breaks in the skin membrane. Anthrax is spread when its spores are inhaled, ingested, or come into contact with skin lesions.

It affects mammals and also certain birds, but mainly cattle, sheep, horses and pigs. It can also affect humans. The risk of spreading to humans though is low.

Cattle and sheep are likely to die quite quickly from the disease, even if they show no signs of it afterwards. The symptoms to be aware of are high temperature, shivering, blood in stool or nostrils, loss of milk, fits, colic, bright fixed expressions and loss of appetite. The symptoms are similar in horses and pigs, though they are likely to be affected by the disease at a slower rate. The only variation may be hot and painful swellings particularly in their throats, and while colic is likely to affect horses only, the loss of appetite is likely to be more prevalent in pigs.

In October 2015, in the first case in Great Britain since 2006, the anthrax disease was found at a farm in Wiltshire in two dead suckler cows. As a result, the farm had all movement restricted and the animal carcasses were also incinerated. Defra encourages the practice of safe biosecurity on all premises with the above livestock in order to ensure outbreaks are minimal and contained.

Aujeszky's disease

Aujeszky's disease affects pigs and is sometimes called by another name, psuedorabies. It has also been known to affect cattle, sheep, cats, dogs and rats. The last known outbreak in Great Britain was in 1989. It is a nervous system condition and is fatal for piglets, usually identified by shivering, loss of co-ordination and a weakening of the hind legs. In adult pigs, it may be recognised by breathing difficulties or severe weight loss. In the other listed animals, it is most commonly seen as an intense rash where the animal will focus on licking and scratching the area to try and relieve the itchiness. They will most likely die within a few days of contracting the disease.

It is spread most commonly though pigs by nose to nose contact, though it is also airborne, hence its presence in other animals. As with the husbandry of all livestock, Defra encourages safe biosecurity.

Intensive farming

Meat and dairy products feature prominently in the British diet. Although carbohydrates (such as pasta and rice) comprise a greater proportion of our diet than they did 10 years ago, we still eat protein in higher quantities than is consumed by our southern European neighbours. We also demand cheap food. The meat, poultry, dairy and egg industries are faced with a choice – to use technological methods in order to keep the price of their products as low as possible, or to allow the animals that they farm to lead more 'natural' lives, which would necessarily reduce yields and increase costs. The use of drugs, hormones and chemicals is almost universal in farming (except in the organic farming movement), as are methods to control the movement of livestock by the use of pens, cages or stalls.

The veterinary profession is faced with a number of difficult decisions. It has to balance the pressure to produce cheap food with its primary aim of maintaining and improving animal welfare. An example of this is the use of antibiotics. Antibiotics are used in farming to treat sick animals. However, they are also used to protect healthy animals against the diseases associated with intensive farming and as growth promoters. The Soil Association reports that about 1,225 tonnes of antibiotics are used each year in the UK, over 60% of which are used for farm animals or by vets. The problem with antibiotics is that bacteria become resistant to them, and overuse of antibiotics in animals has these serious effects:

- resistant strains of bacteria, such as salmonella and *Escherichia coli*, which can be passed on to humans, causing illness and, in extreme cases, death
- bacteria can develop resistance to the drugs that are used to treat serious illness in humans.

Other issues that concern the veterinary profession include:

- the welfare of live farm animals that are exported for slaughter
- battery farming of poultry
- the use of growth hormones
- humane killing of farm animals in abattoirs.

The Protection of Animals Act 1911 contains the general law relating to the suffering of animals, and agricultural livestock is also protected by more recent legislation. New regulations incorporating EU law came into force in August 2000. The regulations cover laying hens, poultry, calves, cattle, pigs and rabbits. More specifically, the EU banned the use of veal crates from 2007 and traditional battery cages from 2012. Details of the regulations can be found on the Defra website (www.defra.gov.uk).

Fox hunting

While not necessarily an issue concerning vets, it is certainly something that you should have an appreciation of as it does concern the animal world. Most people have a view on the issue of hunting with hounds. Prior to the Hunting Act of 2004, there were those, on the one hand, who argued that fox hunting was an integral part of rural life and a countryside tradition, that foxes kill farm animals and therefore need to be controlled, that thousands of rural jobs would be lost if it were banned, and that a ban on fox hunting would lead to a ban on other pastimes, such as shooting and fishing. On the other hand, many people believed that it was a cruel and unnecessary way to control foxes, claiming that around 20,000 foxes were killed every year and that about half that number of hunting dogs were also killed taking part in the sport. Animal rights activists believed it was immoral to chase and kill animals for sport.

The Hunting Act 2004, which banned fox hunting in England and Wales, took effect in February 2005. The Act makes it an offence to hunt a wild mammal with a dog. Nevertheless, some forms of hunting are exempt, including those using no more than two dogs to flush out a mammal to be shot. Controversy on what is a very emotive subject therefore still remains. On the first anniversary of the ban, in February 2006, hunt supporters called for the Act to be repealed, while the League Against Cruel Sports accused 33 hunts of repeatedly breaching the law.

For opposing sides of an argument which continues to be pursued, you should investigate the websites hosted by the League Against Cruel Sports (www.league.uk.com) and the Countryside Alliance (www.countryside-alliance.org). This is a potential topic for conversation because, in 2016, the Conservative Party is committed to pushing ahead with a vote to scrap the law on a fox-hunting ban.

Fall in dairy prices

The UK is the ninth largest milk producer in the world and the third largest in Europe. Although largely (90%) self-sufficient in milk, the UK participates in a significant trade in dairy products. Nevertheless, farmers' unions are warning that the UK dairy industry is facing meltdown unless a national dairy body is established that can regulate farm-gate milk prices.

Milk prices have been low for a number of years and this has been reflected in dairy farm incomes. Prices are expected to fall further as a result of the reform of the Common Agricultural Policy (CAP). Of additional concern to farmers is the fact that some sectors of the supply chain, for example supermarkets, are earning far greater profits than others. As a consequence, some dairy farmers are leaving the industry.

The Dairy Supply Chain Forum is working hard to understand why these farmers are leaving. While it is likely that profitability is an important factor, there are also issues such as succession of ownership and possibilities for diversification that need to be considered. In an open letter to the prime minister, in September 2006, one farm business consultant, David Hughes, referred to the plight of UK dairy farmers as follows:

> 'Today UK milk producers receive approximately 10 pence per pint for milk that costs 11.5 pence per pint to produce. The same milk retails for at least 27 pence per pint in the major supermarkets or up to 48 pence per pint on the doorstep. Production costs have been pared to the bone and there is little or nothing that family farms can do to achieve further savings. Put simply, the balance of power within the supply chain is weighted entirely in favour of the large retailers, with a relatively weak processing sector competing to meet their demands. The individual milk producer

has no bargaining power at all. If society chooses to ignore this gross imbalance of power we will rapidly witness the demise of the family-run dairy farm. They will be replaced by a small number of industrial milk factories that will contribute nothing to our country-side. Worse still, we could end up importing our entire milk supply with all the attendant strategic risks and environmental damage caused by increased food miles.'

In 2012 this remained as much of an issue as ever, and in July 2012 some 2,000 farmers gathered in London to protest about cuts of up to 2p a litre of the overall total they would receive for the milk they sold. In an interview with the BBC, Agriculture Minister Jim Paice gave the example that an average pint of milk cost 49p, of which the dairy farmer received only 16p, which was putting a 'massive burden' on them.

In October 2014, farmers planned protests against the latest dairy cuts, with some farmers then facing revenue cuts of up to 25%. It was reported that there were then 14,000 dairy farms in the UK, producing 3.3 million litres of milk. The cost of production was 30p per litre, with the typical price paid down from 35p per litre in April 2014 to 28p in October 2014.

This worrying trend has continued into 2016, with one in three dairy farms being forced to close in the past three years as a result of super-markets introducing 'mega dairies', as it is cheaper than paying dairy farmers; that is a closure of nearly 1,000 dairy farms.

High Profile Breed (HPB) List for dogs

The Kennel Club is an organisation that advises on issues such as buying and breeding dogs and how best to keep them at home. It also acts as a lobbying committee for issues within the dog world if it believes that tougher action is required to prevent actions that put dogs at risk. In recent years, the European Convention Study Group/2002, set up by the Kennel Club, has identified a number of 'high-profile' breeds of dog, which it defines as:

'A breed from time to time designated by the General Committee as requiring particular monitoring by reason of visible condition(s) which may cause health or welfare concerns.'

These breeds are usually added because someone, whether that be a member of the general public or a professional, has expressed concerns about the health or welfare of the animal. Once the concerns have been identified, the Kennel Club looks closely at the key issues to be addressed within the breed and at health surveys and reviews of the animal, and gets expert opinions on the animal's welfare. The Kennel Club then advises breed clubs on those issues and provides guidance on effective steps to be taken.

At the moment, the current dogs identified in the HPB List are:

- basset hound
- bloodhound
- bulldog
- chow chow
- dogue de Bordeaux (DDB)
- German shepherd dog (GSD)
- mastiff
- Neapolitan mastiff
- Pekingese
- Pug
- St Bernard
- shar pei

NB The Chinese crested, French bulldog and spaniel (cluster) have been removed.

In order to remove a dog from the HPB List, breeders should submit a proposal for their breed to be removed from the list. The committee looks at the recent health survey of the breed, a programme for the ongoing health of the breed, a report from a veterinary surgeon, supporting material from breed clubs, reports and quantitative data with specific veterinary comment, among other things. A formal re-evaluation takes place three years after removal.

Dangerous Dogs Act

The Dangerous Dogs Act, which was introduced in 1991, banned the ownership, breeding, sale and exchange and advertising for sale of specified types of fighting dogs. The dogs covered by the ban included the pit bull terrier. The Act was amended in 1997, one of the effects of which was to lift the mandatory destruction orders that courts applied to dogs found to be of those types listed in the Act. It is now possible, therefore, for prohibited dogs to be added to the Index of Exempted Dogs, but only at the direction of a court and only if the necessary conditions are met (tattooing, microchipping, etc.). No owner may apply to have their dog added to the index – it is entirely a matter for the courts to decide upon. The maximum penalty for illegal possession of a prohibited dog is a fine of £5,000 and/or six months' imprisonment.

Should this issue arise at interview, it is important to demonstrate that you are aware that vicious attacks by certain breeds of unmuzzled dogs on children and adults led to the Act requiring owners to register such dogs with the police and to keep them muzzled.

For the qualified vet, controversy might arise if they are called on to destroy, for example, an unmuzzled pit bull terrier before it has committed an offence. Is such action contrary to the professional oath of a veterinary surgeon? (Privately, many vets say that the Act is unworkable.) If you take a view on this in an interview you will get credit for at least knowing about the law, whether the interviewer agrees with your conclusion or not.

In October 2014, police in Stevenage trialled an education scheme on dangerous dogs after a rise in attacks (from 11 to 31). They stated that if people were more aware of the laws surrounding dangerous animals then these incidents could be avoided. Equally, there needs to be an increased awareness of the change in penalties for owners of dangerous dogs. For example, if a dog attacks and kills an assistance dog, the owner could face up to three years in prison. There are no figures to say whether this has been successful as of yet, though the hope is an increased awareness will lead to a safer environment. Regrettably, there are still many cases of dog violence in the news, with attacks increasing horrendously by around 76% in the last 10 years.

Hybrid dogs

In a consumer-focused society, designer dogs have become the new fad. But does this pose any danger? From labradoodles to puggles, dogs are turning into handbag accessories rather than family pets or functional animals. Originally these designer dogs were designed as a hypo-allergenic version of the guide dog, but the issue of hybrid breeds throws up an ethical question. Hybrid dogs are now sold for staggering amounts of money, and it does raise questions of what hope is there for the adoption of other dogs and for rescue shelters. However, the advantage of breeding designer or hybrid dogs can often be a reduction in the level of genetic defects or health problems found in particular breeds of pedigree dog. The hybrid dog has a much larger genetic pool and therefore a lower risk of suffering from the same health problems of either one of its parents. Hybrid dog breeding remains a controversial topic but one that you should know about and be happy to comment on in terms of both advantages and disadvantages.

Animal testing

Almost all of the drugs used to treat people have been tested on animals. Without rigorous and controlled testing there are significant health risks associated with the use of new medicines. In many cases, the long-term or side effects of drugs can be more serious than the illness itself, and testing is therefore essential. Lord Winston, who pioneered in vitro fertilisation (IVF) and who found wider publicity through his BBC television series *The Human Body*, in response to a report by the House of Lords Select Committee on Science and Technology was quoted in the *Independent* as saying: 'Perceived pressure may persuade people to go down a route which is not going to promote human welfare. We have a major job – animal research is essential for human welfare. Every drug we use is based on it. Without it those drugs would be unsafe.'

Each year British laboratories experiment on approximately 3 million animals. British law requires that any new drug must be tested on at least two different species of live mammal, one of which must be a large non-rodent. UK regulations are considered some of the most rigorous in the world – the Animals (Scientific Procedures) Act 1986 insists that no animal experiments be conducted if there is a realistic alternative.

The debate on animal testing has become a high-profile one because of the activities of animal rights groups. Although the majority of animal rights groups campaign peacefully, the newspapers have given a good deal of publicity to a number of attacks on research laboratories. Huntingdon Life Sciences (HLS), a 60-year-old product development company, was at the forefront of controversy over animal testing. The company claims that it works with a variety of resources, including pharmaceuticals and veterinary products, to help its manufacturers develop safer goods for the market. Some of its opponents claim that HLS kills 500 animals a day in tests for products such as weed killer, food colourings and drugs.

In April 2003, HLS won a High Court injunction preventing protesters going within 50 yards of the homes of staff. In the same month, activists held protests at three colleges of the University of Cambridge against the proposal for a primate experimentation laboratory at Girton College. Oxford University, like HLS, sought to obtain an injunction against animal rights protesters following opposition to a new research laboratory. As with HLS, Oxford was also successful. Protests and demonstrations, however, concerning these cases and other cases of animal testing continue to this day.

Opposition to animal testing is centred on the idea that if animals are similar enough to us for test results to be meaningful, then they are too similar to be experimented upon. Conversely, drugs tested on animals have also gone on to have devastating effects on humans. Examples are the drug thalidomide and the drug trial in March 2006 that caused six men to have multiple organ failure. Campaigners argue that there are alternative methods of testing that do not involve animals. Many of these methods are, they say, also cheaper, quicker and more effective. They include:

- culture of human cells – this is already used in research into cancer, Parkinson's disease and acquired immune deficiency syndrome (AIDS)
- molecular methods, including DNA analysis
- use of micro-organisms
- computer modelling
- use of human volunteers.

Other issues

In addition to the topics listed above, it is advisable for an aspiring vet to have some prior knowledge of other issues that have affected the profession over the past decade. You are also strongly advised to check out the Defra website and look at some of the other global issues affecting animals today, such as African horse sickness, koi herpes virus and West Nile virus.

In the interests of complete exposure, below are note summaries of the current diseases as listed by the World Organisation for Animal Health and Defra. It is not necessarily important that you know about Brucellosis, or even Rift Valley fever, but it is worthwhile having a superficial understanding of them; such as knowing that rinderpest was eradicated worldwide in 2011. For detailed knowledge of each of these, visit the World Organisation for Animal Health, at www.oie.int/animal-health-in-the-world/oie-listed-diseases-2016/ and Defra's notifiable diseases, www.gov.uk/government/collections/notifiable-diseases-in-animals.

African horse sickness, affects horses, does not affect humans; there has never been an outbreak in the UK.

African swine fever, affects pigs, does not affect humans; there has never been an outbreak in the UK.

Brucellosis, there are several different types affecting different animals, it does not affect humans; there was an outbreak in Great Britain in 2004 and it affected cattle.

Chronic wasting disease, affects deer, it has been devastating in Northern America and Canada but it is not known to affect humans; there has never been an outbreak in the UK.

Classical swine fever, affects pigs, it does not affect humans; there has never been an outbreak in the UK.

Contagious agalactia, affects sheep and goats, it does not affect humans; there has never been an outbreak in the UK.

Contagious bovine pleuro-pneumonia, affects cattle, it does not affect humans; there has not been an outbreak in the UK since 1898.

Contagious epididymitis, affects sheep and goats, it does not affect humans; there has never been an outbreak in the UK.

Contagious equine metritis, a disease in all types of equine animals and is usually spread during mating, it does not affect humans; the last known case in the UK was in 2012.

Dourine, a disease in all types of equine animals, it does not affect humans; there has never been an outbreak in the UK.

Enzootic bovine leukosis, affects cattle, spread during pregnancy, during suckling or by animals grouped together; it does not affect humans and the last outbreak in Great Britain was in 1996.

Epizootic haemorrhagic disease, generally considered to affect all animals that chew cud, does not affect humans; there has never been an outbreak in the UK.

Epizootic lymphangitis, principally affects horses and mules (also can affect cattle but that is rare), it is spread by flies and contamination on equipment, it does not affect humans; the last case in Great Britain was in 1906.

Equine infectious anaemia (swamp fever), spread by horse flies, this only affects horses, causes tiredness and fever in the animal, it does not affect humans; the last known case in Great Britain was in 2012.

Equine viral arteritis, spread through mating, this affects equine animals but is only notifiable in stallions and mares, it does not affect humans; the last know case in Great Britain was in 2012.

Glanders and farcy, transmitted through ingestion, either eating or drinking, it affects horses, donkeys and mules, and can also be 'chronic', often lasting for years; it is potentially fatal for humans, with the last case in Great Britain being in 1928.

Goat plague, affects goats and sheep, does not affect humans; there has never been an outbreak in the UK.

Lumpy skin disease, it affects cattle and water buffalo, does not affect humans; there has never been an outbreak in the UK.

Newcastle disease, affects poultry, captive and wild birds, it is spread through the exchange of bodily fluids and it can be harmful to humans, though only in the short term and does not require treatment every time; the last reported case in Great Britain was in 2006.

Paramyxovirus infection, spread as a result of unsanitary conditions for pigeons, it affects the pigeon population and it is not known to be harmful to humans; it is currently a disease present in Great Britain and worthwhile researching.

Porcine epidemic diarrhoea, otherwise known as 'PEDV' and highly infectious, it affects pigs and is currently posing a significant risk to British herds; it does not affect humans.

Rabies, affects all mammals, transmitted in infected animals' saliva and through their bite and can affect humans. The important thing is to look for a change in behaviour in the animal as rabies manifests itself in an animal in different ways; it was eradicated from all mammals in the UK in 1922 but it still exists in bats. A risk is still posed to humans if they are bitten or scratched by a bat.

Rabies in bats, as above but note that the most recent case of rabies in bats in Great Britain was at the time this book went to print in late 2016.

Rift Valley fever, affects sheep, goats, cattle, lambs and humans; there has never been an outbreak in the UK.

Rinderpest, a disease that affects cattle, spread through direct contact and exchange of bodily fluids, although there is no risk to humans; the last known case in Great Britain was in 1877 and it was eradicated from the world stage in 2011.

Scrapie, affects the brains of sheep and goats and is fatal. Two types, classical and atypical, the former being highly contagious, the latter being barely contagious, as a result of which, most of the advice around scrapie is to do with the animal husbandry. If found, often this will lead to a cull of the flock; it has not been proven to affect humans; it is active in the UK.

Sheep and goat pox, as implied, only these animals are in danger of this disease, spread usually through direct contact or insects; there has not been a case in Great Britain since the 1800s.

Sheep scab, a skin condition in sheep alone, passed on by mites through direct contact of the fur; it is very much present in Great Britain today but poses no immediate fatal risk.

Swine vesicular disease, affects pigs, and while it is not common in humans, there have been incidents that have shown that it can accidentally pose a risk to human health. It will mostly be spread through faeces and bodily fluid or by pigs eating infected meat or something else; the last case in Great Britain was in 1982.

Teschen disease, affects sheep, does not affect humans; there has not been a case in Europe since the 1980s.

Vesicular stomatitis, affects cattle, horses, pigs and donkeys, sheep and goats can also be affected but they are more resistant, it does not affect humans; there has never been an outbreak in the UK.

Warble fly, normally affects cattle but also can affect deer and horses too, spread via insects, it does not pose a risk to human health; the disease has not been seen in Great Britain since the 1990s.

West Nile fever, affects many types of animals from cattle to horses, it also affects humans as it is mostly spread by mosquitoes. The symptoms are often a lack of energy and swollen lymph nodes, usually in the neck; birds tend to carry the disease between countries when they migrate; while it is not rife in Great Britain there are some cases to note.

Source for list included above: 'Notifiable diseases in animals' (www.gov.uk/government/collections/notifiable-diseases-in-animals.)

Case study

Are you ever truly prepared for the realities of such a demanding job? This is a very difficult question to answer. Kim qualified from Edinburgh University six years ago and is currently working in general practice.

'You can never underestimate the importance of sound theory and training, but more than that, you can never underestimate the value of experience. I got first-rate training from Edinburgh – the balance between scientific and medical aspects of the course was just right, and the emphasis on the practical side of the profession was invaluable. As a result of the hard work undertaken on the course, I had confidence on graduating that I could handle any likely situation. It is amazing how much more there is to learn upon leaving university, though. It was almost as though the course had merely scratched the surface. This, of course, is not the case, but it is true to say that only by putting the theory into practice can an aspiring vet appreciate what it is like to be a vet.

'It is a job with incredible diversity, and indeed diversity that can change on a knife edge. With all the changes in the industry and the current economic and political climate, which does have an effect on the veterinary world as well, it is of the utmost importance that professionals keep themselves well informed. This can be hard as a vet's hours are long and arduous – but keep your ear to the ground. It is known as continuing professional development (CPD) and it is a requirement of the RCVS. It might seem like the last thing you wish to do after a long week, but CPD allows vets to network with others in the profession through training sessions where we can discuss the updated trends.'

As with many other vets we have heard from, Kim's interest in veterinary science started when she was very young, when she used to go riding with a friend back home in Birmingham. Unlike many others, though, Kim was accepted to veterinary school as a graduate, only arriving at the decision to work in the veterinary profession after first studying for a degree in biology. Having made this decision late, Kim had to take any opportunity in order to gain the relevant work experience, so she appreciates the value of hard work and likes those who undertake work experience with her to display that same drive. Now Kim is working as a veterinary surgeon and hopes to own her own practice in the not-too-distant future.

Importance of the interview

So, those were just a few of the possible questions and issues that you might expect to come up at a selection interview for entry to veterinary school. To be called for interview is a positive sign as it indicates that your application is being considered, and a good interview can lead to an offer. Another reason for trying to do well at the interview stage is that candidates whose grades fall just below those required in their conditional offers are often reconsidered. If places are available, a good interview performance could tip the balance in your favour.

Advice from the admissions tutors:

'Be yourself, as the only way to control your nerves is when you are in control of yourself. We want to meet you. Try and remember we judge you on your body language too so how you come across is important, simply because it will be important when you are actually a vet facing clients.'

'Read your personal statement thoroughly. I lose count of how often students cannot refer back to what they wrote in answers they give to us and it is not our job to spoonfeed you.'

'We are not trying to catch you out, but we are trying to get you to think. Questions can and will be varied but all will be answerable. Some might seem harder than others, however think about what the question is actually asking you and try and give an answer based on that. The key is balance, giving both sides to the argument. If you do not know the answer to a question, please just say that and we will help you. Do not make something up as you will tie yourself in knots. If you would like the question clarifying, please ask as this will not be a detrimental factor in your interview.'

'Practice is important, and you can clearly notice the difference between those who have put in the effort in advance and those who have not. Do not over-prepare as no one wants robotic answers, rather ask fellow applicants and tutors to throw questions at you and make sure they are different each time.'

Demeanour

Most candidates will do their best to prepare well for the interview by anticipating likely questions. However, very few candidates realise that the visual impression they are creating will count for as much as their verbal answers to questions. It is a bit like the old saying, 'It's not what you say, it's the way that you say it.'

Admissions tutors are unlikely to admit that they are going to be influenced by appearance and body language, but they are only human. There is bound to be subjectivity involved. What can you do about it? Try to look your best and try to be as relaxed as possible in what will undoubtedly be a fairly tense situation. Here are a few points to watch.

Body language

When you first enter the room, smile and give a firm handshake. Veterinary schools are friendly places and like to exude informality. Sit comfortably and reasonably upright, leaning forward slightly. This position makes you look and feel alert. Try not to be so tense that you are crouching forward, giving an impression of a panther about to spring. However, do not go to the other extreme of leaning back and looking irritatingly self-assured. Where do you put your hands during the interview? Try resting one on top of the other on your lap. Alternatively, let each hand rest by your side. It is not a good idea to have your arms folded – it looks as though you are shutting the interviewer out.

Speak clearly and deliberately. Do not rush things. When people are nervous they tend to speed up, which makes it harder for the listener. Make eye contact – looking at the person who asked you the question. If it is a panel interview, let your glance take in others at the table, to make them feel that they are included. You should certainly have at least one mock interview, which, if possible, should be recorded on video so that you can see how you come across. You will then be able to spot any mannerisms, such as touching your head or cracking your knuckles, which might distract the interviewers.

Your appearance

Look your best. This does not mean that you should look like a tailor's dummy, but you should wear clothes that are smart, not showy, and in which you feel comfortable. Pay attention to details such as polishing your shoes and washing your hair.

Fact: Dogs can alert their owners of an epileptic seizure up to an hour before it occurs.

8 | A leopard does not change its spots
Non-standard applicants

This book has focused on those students who are applying on a 'standard' application with A levels, IB, Highers, Irish Leaving Certificate or another sixth form equivalent. However, those are not the only qualifications that will be considered. There are a large number of overseas applicants for veterinary medicine each year and this is discussed in this chapter, alongside those wishing to study overseas, mature students and those with special needs.

Overseas students

Despite the EU referendum result on 24 June 2016, EU students are not, at the moment, treated in this bracket. As we will discuss later on, there are currently no changes in their status. What we will do though, is to separate them out in this book from Home/domestic students as the picture may change over time.

The competition for places at veterinary school is high and, as an overseas student, it would be sensible to email an admissions tutor to discuss your application informally with the university before submitting it. If you have not taken A levels or the International Baccalaureate (IB), this does not mean that you will not get a place. However, you do need to have a qualification recognised by English institutions and you need to refer directly to the universities with your specific qualification for advice. Information about qualifications can also be obtained from British Council offices in your country (www.britishcouncil.org). The UCAS website also has a section for international students which describes in detail the application process and deadlines.

BMAT

Other than at Cambridge, as for domestic and EU students, there is no requirement for overseas applicants to sit the BMAT examination.

Fees

Overseas students are liable for the full cost of tuition. Universities do have international scholarships available. For these you apply directly to the university. See Chapter 10 for more information on fees and funding.

English language qualifications

In order to prove your English ability you must pass an English language test. This is for any student who is not a British citizen. The most common test is the IELTS (International English Language Testing System). You should be looking at achieving at least IELTS 7.0 in order to begin the university course and certainly no less than 6.5 in each band. The TOEFL (Test of English as a Foreign Language) exam is largely no longer a Secure English Language Test, as the government declassified it in 2014 as a qualification for testing the English language level of international students. While some universities will continue to accept it as a qualification, the majority will not, and therefore you are safest taking IELTS Academic.

Visas

International students will have to apply for a Tier 4 Student Visa before they are able to study in the UK. In order to get a Tier 4 Student Visa you will need a CAS (Confirmation of Acceptance for Studies) from the individual university which made the offer. In order to get a CAS, you will need to show various documents as set out by the admissions department. This can take time – there is no way of saying how much time as that will vary from country to country, but it can be days or weeks. The important thing is for you to apply for a CAS as soon as you are able.

Studying outside the UK

An option for students who wish to study overseas, but want to undertake some of their clinical training in one of the UK veterinary schools, is the veterinary science course offered by St George's University in Grenada, West Indies. Another place that may be of interest is the Faculty of Medicine at Kosice, Slovak Republic, where the course is taught in English and accredited by the RCVS. For contact details for the course, see Chapter 12.

It is possible to practise as a vet in the UK having studied overseas; details are given on the RCVS website. You should ultimately check in advance though that your qualification will be accepted as a licence to practice veterinary medicine in Great Britain. The process is simpler for students who have studied in certain universities in Canada, Australia,

South Africa or New Zealand where their degrees are approved by the RCVS. Currently, students who have studied in the EU can also register with the RCVS if they have EU community rights entitlement (entitlement rights to work in a member state). In the wake of Brexit, this may change as a result of the UK's future negotiations with the EU. More information can be found on the RCVS website at www.rcvs.org.uk/ news-and-events/news/rcvs-holds-the-first-meeting-of-its-brexit-presidential.

Graduates from other countries can still practise in the UK if they pass the statutory examination for membership of the RCVS, which is held in a UK veterinary school in May/June each year. Further information for all overseas graduates can be obtained from the RCVS website (www.rcvs.org.uk).

Mature students

A mature applicant is someone who is 21 years old or more on the first day of their studies.

In view of the extreme competition for places, it is unrealistic for mature students, at, say, 25 or 30 years of age, to expect special treatment. They should expect to satisfy the academic entry requirements in the usual way at one recent sitting and must have a good range of practical experience. However, this requirement has been known to be waived in exceptional cases, such as where a mature student displays strong motivation coupled with academic ability.

Mature applicants should use the personal statement section of the UCAS application to set out their qualifications and work experience. Your objective is to signal to the admissions tutors why they should see you. Your extra maturity and practical experience should show here. If you cannot get all the information in the space allowed, make sure you summarise what you want to get across in accordance with the bullet points in Chapter 6 (see pages 77–78) – why you want to study veterinary science, what you have done to explore this decision, how you respond to people, how you react under pressure, what your career aspirations are, and what your extracurricular interests are – in order to show that you are a rounded individual.

Remember, it is very important to show why you want to work with animals and to give details of any relevant work experience of a paid or voluntary nature. If you feel that the space in the personal statement section of the UCAS application does not permit you to do full justice to yourself, it is a good idea to prepare a CV or further documentation and send this directly to the veterinary school with your UCAS application number.

Students with disabilities and special educational needs

Students with disabilities and special educational needs are welcome at all institutions and are not disadvantaged. If you have a disability or health condition, you are encouraged to look at the demands of the course at the individual university. Those with a hearing or visual impairment are equally encouraged to apply. The institutions are fully committed to support students with additional needs, from dyslexia to physical disability, and have access arrangements in place. It is advisable in each situation to contact the universities individually and explain to them your circumstances as well as including details on the UCAS form. The more information you can give them, the better they will be able to advise you on what arrangements are in place. Provisions are usually made within the teaching facilities; some forms of accommodation may pose more of a logistical problem.

In terms of special educational needs, students who require a word processor or extra time will be allowed these in the same way that they would have been at school, subject to providing the correct documentation to the university.

For more information, refer directly to the university, which will probably have a person in charge of special access arrangements.

Fact: A cat can be either right-pawed or left-pawed.

9 | A bird in the hand
Results day

It is August and the dreaded results day. No matter how much preparation went in, there will always be nerves on the day. The best case scenario is, of course, that you meet the grade requirements for your offer. In that situation you can check your UCAS Track and see that your offer has been made unconditional. The next step is for the university to contact you directly. However, you need to be prepared for other scenarios in case the results do not match your predictions.

What to do if you have good grades but no offer

There are a number of students who will approach results day without having received an offer from a veterinary school. In the past, if you found yourself in this position and secured excellent grades in your A levels, it might have been possible to find a place through Clearing. Unfortunately, it is now virtually impossible for a student to secure a place on a veterinary course in this way, even if they hold outstanding grades. This situation is unlikely to change in coming years. Ultimately, though, Clearing may be of use to secure a place on an alternative course.

If you hold three A or A* grades but were rejected when you applied through UCAS (i.e. you did not get an offer), you need to let the veterinary schools know that you are out there, and discuss options for how you may secure a place in the future. The best way to do this is by phone or email directly. They will be busy on results day, so bear with the institutions around that time. There is no substitute for establishing a good rapport with an admissions tutor – they will be able to give you guidance on exactly what you need to do next and what they are looking for.

The most likely scenario is that you will have to reapply through UCAS in the next admissions cycle. Although you will already have the grades for entry in this situation, it is important to understand that there are a number of other elements of your application that you'll need to work on to maximise your chances of securing a place. Things to consider are listed below.

- Your personal statement – revisit it and cast a critical eye over it. This is also an opportunity to add in any work placements or other positive experiences that you have had since your last application.

- Your BMAT score – if you are applying to Cambridge, you will need to resit your BMAT for each admissions cycle. This will give you a chance to complete further practice questions and learn from your experience of sitting it first time around. It may also be a good idea to attend one of the BMAT preparation courses that are available.
- Your work experience – any opportunity to add further work experience to your profile will always be a good step. Whether it is veterinary-related or just general voluntary work, it will have a positive impact. That said, focus on applying for veterinary places as much as you can as this will show you are still focused on this course despite the setback.

UCAS Adjustment

There is a system called UCAS Adjustment that allows applicants who pass their exams with better results than expected to get a place at a higher-level university. However, this is not likely to be the case for veterinary school as they all require high grades and you would not have been made an offer that required lower grades. You can enter Adjustment only if your results have met and exceeded the conditions of your conditional firm choice. A student must have held a conditional firm choice on their application to be eligible, and so, if you have had no offers, it is not something you can use. In short, Adjustment doesn't help if you have applied to veterinary schools.

What to do if you hold an offer but miss the grades

If you have only narrowly missed the required grades, it is important that you contact the admissions team as soon as possible. As mentioned previously, you will probably know what their decision is at this point, thanks to the UCAS website. If you have been rejected, it is vital that you keep a level head and do not panic; you must stay calm throughout. If you have not been rejected outright or are unsure of their decision, you must contact the admissions team by telephone – so ensure that in the run-up to results day you have gathered together the contact numbers of the universities you have accepted as your firm and insurance choices.

In some cases, veterinary schools will allow applicants who hold a conditional offer to slip a grade (particularly if they came across well at the interview stage) rather than offering the place to somebody else. It will depend by how much you have missed the grade – with uniform mark scale (UMS) points nowadays that is easy to ascertain. However, be warned – this is a rare occurrence and most of the time dropping a grade will result in outright rejection.

When speaking to the universities, they are likely to give you a simple yes or no answer or tell you that you are still being considered. It is unlikely that crying, begging or pleading your case to the person on the phone will make any difference to the overall decision. If they tell you that you have been rejected, there are some questions you should ask.

- Would they consider your application if you applied next year (i.e. do they accept resit students)?
- What would the likely grade requirements be? (They will almost certainly ask for at least AAA, but it is worth checking anyway.)
- Would they interview you again?

If at all possible, get something in writing to refer to when reapplying.

Retaking A levels

Many unsuccessful candidates decide to do a repeat year and take their examinations again. Before doing this it would be sensible to seek the advice of an admissions tutor. The fact is that not many people doing repeats are made unconditional offers unless there are documented extenuating circumstances, such as serious illness. If you are made an offer it will usually be based upon the second attempt and the requirement could be raised to achieving one grade higher than the published offer across the three subjects. You may get a repeat offer if you have narrowly failed to secure a place on the first try and are excellent in all other respects.

The truth is that the almost overwhelming pressure of demand from highly motivated and well-qualified candidates is taking its toll on the chances of those repeating A levels. Selection is becoming more stringent, resulting in fewer resitters being successful. However, you are still encouraged to do so.

Retakes are considered by universities depending on the specific policy of the institution you are applying to. In most cases the policy is that students can retake without penalty; however, you must achieve the offer grades in the second sitting. There can also be a condition placed on you that you have to have achieved a minimum grade in a specific subject at AS. Retakes within a two-year course are accepted without problem. The RVC states in their Admissions Policy, 'The College welcomes applications to our veterinary medicine degrees from applicants who are resitting whole or parts of their qualifications' (www.rvc.ac.uk/Media/Default/About/Academic%20Quality,%20Regulations%20and%20Procedures/General/admissions-policy-taught-courses.pdf).

Most universities say that you must complete the qualification within two years and one re-sit is allowed, though if this takes place in a third year, the entry requirement will increase. Edinburgh on the other hand says it will not accept anything other than students who have achieved the grades required in the first sitting as competition is so fierce. That said, overall, you can generally consider that two applications will be considered but you will be fighting with first-time applicants.

In the new linear system of A levels, a re-sit will only be possible of the whole A level, and this will take place in May to June of each year.

An A* is achieved by averaging 90% overall, although this is still to be clarified by Ofqual. Sixth-form colleges are usually happy to advise students about their options.

Reapplying

In order to reapply, you have to go through exactly the same process again, taking into account all that has been said above. However, when reapplying, make sure you update your application. A careless application would be one that does not include anything new about what you have planned – and worse, it does not update a personal statement!

Make sure that you talk to admissions tutors about your chances before you reapply, as they may suggest that you take a three-year degree in a related subject, Bioveterinary Science for example, and then apply for graduate entry. It is important to take their opinion on board as they are the ones who will be making the decision.

If you had extenuating circumstances first time round, then mention them at this point but make sure they are compelling – not just 'I had a cold on the day'!

Often it is better to reapply once you have your resit grades, even though this might mean waiting another year.

Fact: Chocolate is poisonous to both cats and dogs. Surprisingly though, it is the most effective type of mice bait – mice don't really like cheese that much at all!

10 | Counting sheep
Financing your course

Once you arrive in veterinary school, you will want at least to avoid the worry of getting too deeply into debt. Money is a problem for all students and those studying veterinary science will have additional expenses connected with their course, mainly travel expenses, clothing, books and equipment. Veterinary students are also limited in the opportunities they have to earn extra money during the holidays because they have to spend time doing EMR/EMS to gain the prescribed experience in veterinary practice as part of their training. Students believe that sixth-formers and others preparing to go to veterinary school should be forewarned about coping with the money side of being a veterinary student.

First-year expenditure for veterinary students is particularly high and can easily exceed £9,000 for those living away from home.

Fees

UK students

From September 2017, universities will be allowed to charge UK and EU students up to £9,250 a year for tuition fees as part of the government's new Teaching Excellence Framework (TEF), which will assess universities and colleges on the quality of their teaching. The higher-ranked universities will be able to charge the maximum amount (£9,250), though they are not unanimous in terms of when and whether they will effect this. Tuition fee loans will increase to cover the higher fees. The fee cap for students studying in Wales remains at £9,000, while fees for students in Northern Ireland have yet to be confirmed for 2017 entry. You should refer to the websites of the specific universities to find out what they intend to charge, and also to the UCAS website – use the course search facility.

If you are a student whose main residence is in England, you will pay up to £9,000 if you study in Wales, and up to £9,250 in the rest of the UK.

If you are a student whose main residence is in Scotland and meet eligibility requirements, the Student Awards Agency Scotland (SAAS) will pay your fees if you study at a Scottish university. You will pay up to £9,000 if you study in Wales and up to £9,250 in England and Northern Ireland, and you can apply for a loan from the SAAS to cover part or all of the fees.

If you are a student whose main residence is in Wales, you will pay up to £4,046 if you study in Wales, and up to £9,250 if you study in the rest of the UK; however, you will be able to receive a £4,296 loan from the Welsh government, and you will also be eligible for a grant up to the difference between the loan and the full fee.

If you are a student whose main residence is in Northern Ireland, you will pay up to £9,000 if you study in Wales and up to £9,250 if you study in England or Scotland, but only £3,925 if you study in Northern Ireland.

EU students

If you are an EU student, you will pay up to £9,250 if you study in England, but no fee if you study in Scotland. If you study in Wales you will pay up to £4,046 and will receive the same help as Welsh students (see above) subject to the current EU terms. If you study in Northern Ireland, you will pay up to £3,925. See Table 3 below.

Implications of Brexit

With Britain voting to leave the European Union, many universities were concerned about what that would mean for European student numbers at each institution. Prime Minister Theresa May announced in autumn 2016 that she intends to trigger Article 50 of the Lisbon Treaty by the end of March 2017, which will launch the process of formally negotiating Britain's exit from the EU. Therefore, for the time being, until it is announced otherwise, EU students will continue to pay the same fees as Home students. EU students starting their course in September 2017 will pay Home fees for the duration of their course. More importantly, EU students starting their courses in September 2017 remain eligible to apply for student funding under the current terms. This was confirmed by Jo Johnson, Minister for Universities and Science, in September 2016.

Table 3 Annual tuition fees by region for courses starting in 2017

Student's home region	Studying in England	Studying in Scotland	Studying in Wales	Studying in Northern Ireland (2016)*
England	Up to £9,250	Up to £9,250	Up to £9,000	Up to £9,250
Scotland	Up to £9,250	No fee	Up to £9,000	Up to £9,250
Wales	Up to £9,250	Up to £9,250	Up to £4,046	Up to £9,250
Northern Ireland	Up to £9,250	Up to £9,250	Up to £9,000	Up to £3,925
EU	Up to £9,250	No fee	Up to £4,046	Up to £3,925
Other international	Variable	Variable	Variable	Variable

*2017 fee levels for Northern Ireland are yet to be confirmed.
Source: www.ucas.com. We acknowledge UCAS' contribution of this information.

International student fees

Students from outside the EU pay more in tuition fees than UK or EU students. The fees for non-EU international students do not have a set upper limit. The fees will depend on the course and the university. The fees at the RVC are £33,000 per year for pre-clinical and clinical training (based on figures provided by the RVC for 2017–18). However, the figure for Bristol is £19,400 for the pre-clinical stage of the course, rising to £35,400 in the clinical stage.

Funding

Loans

A non-means-tested tuition fees loan is available for tuition fees up to £9,250. This will be paid by the Student Loans Company and will be added to your overall loan. Your repayments are deferred until after you have left university and have started earning £21,000 or more per year.

A maintenance loan (student loan) is different from a tuition fees loan. This is a variable, means-tested loan designed to aid with living costs. The table below shows what you are entitled to borrow.

Table 4 Expected maintenance loan for 2017

Location	Maximum loan
London	£11,002
Elsewhere	£8,430
Parental home	£7,097

The above figures refer to students from England. Figures from other parts of the UK will vary slightly; for more details, visit the UCAS website.

Grants

As of September 2016, maintenance grants are no longer available in England; they have been replaced by maintenance loans. Students from other parts of the UK can apply for grants to help with living costs provided they meet the eligibility requirements. For further details please refer to the UCAS website www.ucas.com and to the student funding website for your country.

England: Student Finance England www.gov.uk/contact-student-finance-england

Wales: Student Finance Wales www.studentfinancewales.co.uk

Scotland: Student Awards Agency for Scotland www.saas.gov.uk

Northern Ireland: Student Finance NI www.studentfinanceni.co.uk

Bursaries

The veterinary schools offer bursaries and further advice on sources of funding. You should read the websites of the universities in order to find out whether you will be able to get a reduction in fees. The University of Liverpool, for example, offers a means-tested bursary (see Table 5 below). The table is an example of what students studying at Liverpool were able to receive in 2016/17.

Table 5 Students studying outside London and living away from the parental home

Household income (up to)	Amount parents/partner expected to contribute	Maintenance loan	Liverpool bursary*	Total (maintenance loan & Liverpool bursary)
£25,000	£0	£8,200	£2,000	£10,200
£30,000	£0	£7,162	£750	£8,362
£35,000	£0	£7,023	£750	£7,773
£40,000	£0	£6,434	£0	£6,434
£42,870	£0	£6,095	£0	£6,095
£45,000	£250	£5,845	£0	£5,845
£50,000	£839	£5,256	£0	£5,256
£55,000	£1,428	£4,667	£0	£4,667
£60,000	£2,017	£4,078	£0	£4,078
£62,180 and over	£2,274	£3,821	£0	£3,821

Source: https://www.liverpool.ac.uk/study/undergraduate/finance/scholarships/liverpool-bursary/.
Reproduced with the kind permission of the University of Liverpool.
* Subject to approval from Office of Fair Access (OFFA).
Figures are correct for 2016/17 entry.

Armed Forces bursaries are grants to selected veterinary students who pass their Army Officer Selection Board examinations and apply before their final university year. In return, you have to spend four years in the service. For more details, have a look online at www.army.mod.uk/join/20109.aspx.

International students

There is not a lot of funding available from universities for international students so you must make sure you have the funding in place already. Options can be found though and there are some scholarships available, though they are not plentiful. For example, the RVC offers a fully funded, fees-waived scholarship for *one* international student. There are also examples of associations in country of origin offering scholarships; the Agri-Food and Veterinary Authority of Singapore

(AVA), for example, offers students financial assistance. International bursaries are available (based on the admissions process, where they consider academic strengths and means-tested conditions) to the value of one year's tuition fees. While you need to look at each university separately, have a look at the RVC website as an example of what is available (www.rvc.ac.uk/Undergraduate/Finances.cfm). Depending on where you are applying from, you should get in touch with the British Council in your country and find out what funding is available for you to study overseas. There is often funding available from a variety of sources within each country.

Students are able to apply for student loans by selecting option 02 (for local government authority) on the UCAS form under 'Fees and Funding'. You can also apply to the Student Loans Company for a loan. Find out more at www.slc.co.uk.

You should also visit the BVA website to find out more about sources of funding for veterinary students: www.bva.co.uk/public/documents/funding_sources.pdf.

Keeping costs down: hints and tips

- Avoid buying lots of kit or textbooks in advance. When you get to the course you may find some discounts are offered. Second-hand textbooks may be for sale, although many veterinary students prefer to keep their textbooks for use in their working lives. Also try medical students for second-hand textbooks.
- Check for student travel concessions and get advice on the best offers on the regular trips that you will have to make.
- Apply early for the student loan, as it takes some time for the loan to be processed. Remind the bank about that overdraft facility it promoted to you when it sought your custom.
- Veterinary students work hard and like to play hard as well. Set yourself a limit on how much you are prepared to spend each term. Remember: the more partying, the worse your bank account will look. Perhaps you will go to the annual vet ball; if you do, why not consider buying a second-hand outfit? By all means join the Association of Veterinary Students (AVS), but do you want to attend the congress or go on sports weekends? They all cost money.
- Easter is a time when it is possible for students to augment their income. Once you have gained experience with your first lambing, students say that it is possible, if you are lucky, to make over £300 per week. This is very hard work, involving 12 hours a day, for seven days a week, for a minimum of three weeks. But it will certainly improve your bank account – and give you valuable experience.

Expected student expenditure

The two lists below show the estimated additional course costs (2016/17) for students applying to veterinary science courses at the University of Cambridge.

Veterinary Medicine (pre-clinical)

Lab coat	£10.00
Dissection kit, gloves, safety glasses, loan of locker and key, loan of dog skeleton	£24.00
Veterinary Dissection Manual, which includes course guides for Veterinary Anatomy and Physiology (1st Year) and Neurobiology and Comparative Veterinary Biology (2nd Year)*	£14.00
Wellington boots (with toe-protector)	£12.00
University-approved calculator	£14.00–£16.00
Electron micrographs (optional)	£ 3.00
EMS (pre-clinical) 12 weeks' practical vacation experience with animals, particularly farm animals. Insurance cover provided but no subsistence grants payable	Variable

Veterinary medicine (clinical)

Locker padlock	£6.85
Clinical thermometer	£3.36
Digital thermometer	£4.50
6" scissors curved on flat	£2.42
Spencer Wells Forceps 5"	£3.05
Pen torch	£1.44
Dog lead (red)	£1.26
Overalls	£16.74
Hoof pick	£0.69
Yard boots	(not stocked by vet department store)
Stethoscope (this is a basic level stethoscope; many students purchase a higher quality stethoscope later in the clinical course)	£2.35
EMS – 26 weeks required by RCVS – variable depending on chosen placements (grants are available to assist with costs)	
BVA insurance cover, at a cost of £39.00 per annum, will be met by the Veterinary School	

Source for both tables: http://www.biology.cam.ac.uk/undergrads/mvst/prospective-students/cost. Reproduced with kind permission from the department of Veterinary Medicine at the University of Cambridge.

In addition to the two lists opposite, students will be required to purchase white theatre shoes and protective clothing to be worn in theatre, prior to starting their **6th year rotations**:

White theatre shoes	£1.95 (approximate price)
Theatre scrubs	£12.20 (approximate price)
Stethoscope (advanced)	£100.00

Table 6, below, outlines the estimated expenditure for students for each pre-clinical year, living in London, at home or away from home, factoring in a potential fees rise in 2017.

Table 6 Expenditure estimate per pre-clinical year

Expenses	Living in London away from home	Living outside London away from home	Living at home
Tuition fees	Up to £9,000 per year*	Up to £9,250 per year	Up to £9,250 per year
Overalls	£17	£13.50	£13.50
Lab coats	£10	£8.50	£8.50
Wellies	£12	£12	£12
Course notes	£75	£75	£75
Textbooks	£300	£300	£300
Rent	£6,143	£4,834	N/A
Food	£1,956	£1,956	Variable
Household	£316	£316	Variable
Insurance	£65	£42	Variable
Personal	£2,074	£2,074	Variable
Travel	£1,524	£1,524	£1,524
Leisure	£1,310	£1,310	£1,310
Total	**£22,802**	**£21,720**	**Variable**

Key
* Tuition fees for 2017 – RVC has said it is charging £9,000 though this might rise. Others outside London, such as Bristol, have already declared for £9,250, so these are generalised estimates.

Scottish students are not expected to pay the £1,820 tuition fee if this is their first degree; if eligible, the government in Scotland pay that fee, subject to conditions.

Note: These figures, aside from the tuition fees which are applicable as of 2017–18 entry, were estimated in October 2016 and are intended only as a guide. Therefore, please refer to university websites for a detailed breakdown of the individual expenditure requirements.

Figures for rent, food, household, insurance, personal, travel and leisure sourced from the NUS, www.nus.org.uk/en/advice/money-and-funding/average-costs-of-living-and-study.

Case study

Jade is 23 and currently studying at the University of Surrey. She did well in her A levels but was unsure of what she wanted to study at university, so took a year out before eventually deciding to go down the route of veterinary medicine.

'I finished sixth form with good grades in English, History and Politics but I had no idea what to do at uni so I went straight into work. During my year out I managed to secure not only a retail job but also voluntary experience at a local animal shelter and it was then that I realised that I really wanted to be a vet. It had been a dream of mine as a child that I thought I'd grown out of, but apparently not!'

Jade spent three months volunteering in the kennels before eventually also taking up animal fostering.

'It was my love of animals that initially drew me in and ultimately became the decisive factor in my choice of degree. Unfortunately I didn't have A levels in any sciences so I took intensive courses in biology and chemistry (gaining As in both) before I then applied to Surrey to study veterinary medicine and science. It wasn't the most straightforward of routes but I'm glad things went the way that they did. I'm also really pleased that I took the time out to work and volunteer because I was able to really think about what course I wanted to do and do my research rather than rush into three or more years of study in something I wasn't really passionate about.'

Now well into her first year, Jade is finding her feet.

'My course is amazing but it is definitely hard work. I did two weeks of calving during my Easter break which was a great experience. I was really nervous going into it as I had heard that most farmers don't think women are capable of working with large animals but that wasn't my experience at all. The farmers were all incredibly helpful and let me get really stuck in. I don't think I'll be moving to the countryside any time soon, but I have a two-week placement on a pig farm coming up so you never know!'

Fact: A puppy is born blind, deaf, and toothless.

11 | Snakes and ladders
Career paths

There may be hidden expenses in training to be a vet, but at least you can reflect, with some optimism, that a degree in veterinary science is going to result in a professional qualification and a job. According to figures published in the RCVS's annual RCVS Facts report for 2014 (the last published date), over 87.3% of registered surgeons were in practice and roughly 73.3% of those were in the UK (new data was due to be published in December 2016, but had not been released by the time this book went to press in February 2016).

While in the past few years there has been cause for concern over a shortage of practising vets, the situation now is not as drastic as it has been. In 2011, veterinary surgeons were removed from the national jobs shortage list, which highlights areas of concern in terms of skilled jobs. That said, there is a genuine concern that we have an impending shortage of vets with farm experience, which could leave the UK vulnerable to outbreaks of disease in livestock.

Professional Development Phase

Once you have graduated from your veterinary degree course, you are still not there yet. The year after graduation is known as the Professional Development Phase (PDP), during which you will be expected to develop your skills. The RCVS has developed a set of 'Year-One competences' so that you can record your progress. After that you will always be expected to keep up with your CPD by attending courses and lectures and networking.

Once you have qualified, you might wish to consider working in the types of practice or roles described in this chapter.

Career opportunities

The universities' first-destination statistics show that nearly all veterinary graduates begin their careers in practice, but such is the variety of opportunity in this profession that career change and divergence can and do occur. For example, graduates are employed in government service dealing with investigation, control and eradication of diseases.

There are also opportunities for veterinary scientists to become engaged in university teaching and research establishments at home and abroad.

If you start in general practice, there is the chance to move into different types of practice. The trend is towards small-animal practices, but there is also more opportunity to work with horses – now seen as an important part of the growing leisure industry. There is also a growing trend towards specialisation within practices. Areas of specialisation include cattle, horses, household pets and even exotics. Specialisation can also be more sophisticated – for example, combining equine care with lameness in all animals. Dermatology, soft tissues and cardiology are examples of the kinds of specialisation that are seen as helpful to clients. It is possible for postgraduate specialist qualifications to be obtained through the RCVS's specialist certificate and diploma examinations.

Postgraduate courses

Education in the field of veterinary medicine is continuous; not only that, as a profession, it places a high emphasis on CPD. It is incredibly important to keep yourself up to date and also educate yourself on the variety of different jobs available to you, as the degree course itself – while comprehensive – is not exhaustive, as it cannot be. There are both full-time and part-time postgraduate courses, and they can focus on anything from the welfare of animals to infectious diseases to education. These programmes are designed for anyone looking to advance their knowledge of a specialist part of the profession through research. The postgraduate courses are not restricted to the eight veterinary schools but are available in a range of universities; you can take postgraduate courses in anything from Applied Animal Behaviour and Welfare at Newcastle University to Aquatic Veterinary Studies at the University of Stirling. Courses vary in length depending on whether you are doing the self-study option or a taught one-year course. It is a big factor to consider, i.e. whether you can take a full year off financially or, as with most professionals, to study alongside working.

It is important to note that you do not need a postgraduate course in order to get employment in the profession. These courses are for those who wish to specialise or move into a niche field, such as aquatic veterinary medicine.

These courses have their obvious benefits, i.e. they will allow you to specialise in specific areas of the profession. It is often advised though that you spend some time working as a professional first after your clinical years. It is wise to take a step back and assess your options once you have completed training before making any decisions on your career course.

Veterinary variety: types of vet

With more registered vets than in recent years and an increase in the number of new registrations, the veterinary field still has its problems as a result of the recession. Pet owners are feeling the pinch, which in turn impacts on vets. Smaller vet practices are facing competition from big corporations with marketing budgets, making it harder for them to compete. As your degree progresses, you will most likely find an area of veterinary medicine that you particularly enjoy or have a certain flair for. Before you reach that stage, though, it is worthwhile considering which area immediately strikes you as something to which you feel you could dedicate the next 40 years of your working life.

However, it is highly advisable to start your career in general practice, working with household animals or even with larger animals on a farm, before perhaps opting to specialise in one of the more diverse forms of veterinary surgery.

Small-animal vet

The last RCVS survey in 2010 revealed that about 40.1 hours of a vet's standard working week in a small-animal practice are spent with small animals. This is the most common type of vet, and works in local practice dealing with the care and treatment of household pets. You will be concerned with anything from vaccinations to neutering, as well as local surgery and general health check-ups. In unfortunate situations, you may be required to make the decision as to the kindness of putting an animal down to end its pain.

Large-animal vet

Principally concerned with multiple animals in a group as opposed to individual animals, a large-animal vet is most often found on a farm, and is concerned with the health and productivity of the herd. Your responsibilities are likely to involve the treatment of disease and giving advice on the husbandry of the animals, including nutritional balance and sanitation. This role requires a strong will and a thick skin when dealing with farmers, who are an entirely different clientele to the ordinary public. Once you have the respect and confidence of the farmer, your job will be far easier.

Equine vet

As the name suggests, equine vets specialise in the treatment of horses. Stable and horse owners alike prefer to use a specialist equine vet when it comes to the treatment of their animals because horses are different from other animals in all respects – from anatomy to pharmacology. Horses also require different husbandry and, therefore, as a specialist you will be giving a different form of advice. Before specialising in this area, it is essential, or at least highly advisable, that you gain experience in general practice and then progress to achieving your specialist qualifications later on, once you have general experience to your name.

Exotic-animal vet

Exotic-animal vets have specialist training in the treatment of exotic animals including snakes and turtles. The term 'exotic' is wide ranging, and it is worth remembering that ferrets and small rodents are included in this category. As with an equine vet, becoming a general vet first is a prerequisite to taking your specialist qualifications. There is an element of glamour in this work and you can expect to find yourself spending a lot of time at a zoo working with wild animals.

A rise in the number of exotic animals being kept as pets has meant that there is a new angle being promoted within vet student training. The Hospital for Small Animals at The Royal (Dick) School in Edinburgh has led the way by opening a specialist exotic unit for veterinary student training.

Avian vet

Avian vets are concerned with the treatment of birds, and this specialisation offers you a varied working environment. One day might be spent in private practice, the next in a bird sanctuary and the next in a zoo. You would certainly never be bored! However, you should take prior work in general small-animal practice before specialising with the requisite qualifications, as working with smaller animals will help you appreciate the smaller anatomical size of a bird.

Advice: Usually you need to have a couple of years post-graduation experience before you can – or should – start a qualification to specialise in exotic or avian veterinary medicine.

Other types of vet

The vets listed above are the most common types of veterinary surgeons in the UK. However, this list is by no means comprehensive and, should you wish to, you can also specialise in the following areas:

- cardiology (work based on the study of an animal's heart)
- dairy (work specifically with dairy farmers)
- dental (mouth-based work, including teeth, gums and hygiene)
- diagnostic imaging (to work with MRI and CT scanning)
- feline (working with cats, large and small, including zoo-based work)

- holistic (emphasises the study of all aspects of an animal's health, including physical, psychological, social, economic and cultural factors)
- marine (caring for marine-based animals, such as dolphins and whales – strong swimming ability is a prerequisite).

The veterinary practice

There are many different types of veterinary practice. The majority, however, deal with all species. Others tend to specify the size of the animal, i.e. some deal solely with large animals, some small, and others only equine. The size of practices varies a great deal. The average size is three or four vets working together, but a few are smaller or much larger. Some are incredibly busy, while others may manage to convey an easier atmosphere while being equally hard working. Some practices offer particular facilities which define them as different types of veterinary practice.

The structure of a general practice

In a general practice, a veterinary surgeon is responsible for all types of treatment, from medical to surgical, of all animals. It is not uncommon for veterinary surgeons to study for further qualifications offered by the RCVS while working in order to further their knowledge about certain animals. Veterinary surgeons are vital to the practice and most start as a locum or an associate. Most practices are partnerships run by several veterinary surgeons with one principal. The goal of most associates working in a practice is to reach partnership level. This then involves separate business skills in order to ensure that the practice is making money.

The principal, or practice manager, is usually found in a larger practice as it is important to have one person who has a general overview of the business. This person will be responsible for ensuring that all monies are paid and that the practice is run to a high standard. This role is not common to all practices, as many cannot afford an extra level of support.

From a veterinary surgeon's point of view, the most important people within the practice are veterinary nurses. They ensure that standards of care are high and that both animals and owners are kept comfortable. They assist in supportive care, and also undertake minor surgical procedures and tests, should they be required.

The receptionists are the first point of contact within a practice. A lot of owners will be very disturbed when bringing their animal to the vet and it is the receptionist's responsibility to present a calm and professional approach that will reassure the clients. They are also gatekeepers and personal assistants for the veterinary surgeons, making sure that appointments are managed and schedules are adhered to.

Veterinary practice as a small business

A veterinary practice is dependent upon the income it makes, which is generated by the surgery itself, in order to be a successful small business. It does not receive money from an external source, such as the government. The practice's income is used to pay the staff and the rent (if the site is not owned by the practice) and then the rest is put back into the business to pay for equipment and up-to-date technology.

Vets are often faced with a moral dilemma when seeing a client who cannot afford to pay the veterinary fees for their services. Fees can often be very high and many clients (who are used to human healthcare often being free of charge) are shocked by what they are required to pay for the treatment of their pets. Vets need to be understanding in this sort of situation, but it's important to remember that you are part of a business and this is your livelihood.

Accreditation

All practices need to adhere to the codes of practice of a specific regulatory body.

RCVS accredited practice

The RCVS Practice Standards Scheme was launched on 1 January 2005. It is the only scheme representing the veterinary profession and is a regulatory body set up to ensure the highest standards. If you were to work in an RCVS-accredited practice, you would be dedicated to maintaining the highest possible standard of veterinary care; to providing a greater amount of information regarding the care of animals to the public and to clients; and to being at the cutting edge of advancements within the field of veterinary science.

BEVA listed practice

The British Equine Veterinary Association (BEVA) has compiled a list of self-certified practices in the equine industry and has a code of practice for veterinary surgeons in this field.

AVMA accredited course

The American Veterinary Medical Association is the North American accrediting council for veterinary surgeons. However, in order to practise medicine in North America, students must pass the North American Veterinary Licensing Examination (NAVLE).

EAEVE

The European Association of Establishments for Veterinary Education (EAEVE) currently provides assurance of the veterinary degree in Europe and its standards; the RVC and universities of Copenhagen, Helsinki and Zurich/Bern are the only establishments that currently hold full accreditation.

Government service

In the public sector, vets are involved in protecting public health, working in government departments and agencies such as the Animal Health and Veterinary Laboratories Agency (AHVLA), the Food Standards Agency and the Veterinary Medicines Directorate. Defra employs vets to monitor animal health and to prevent the spread of diseases.

Most of the veterinary surgeons employed by Defra work in the AHVLA. Field officers have a wide range of responsibilities, which include the control of major epidemic diseases of farm animals, matters of consumer protection (largely in relation to meat hygiene), the control of import and export of animals and the operation of health schemes.

The AHVLA comprises officers who are based in laboratories. Their job is to operate and support control schemes in the interests of public health, to monitor developments and give early warning of any disease problems or dangers to the safety of the food chain. They also provide practising vets with a chargeable diagnostic service. The Veterinary Laboratories Agency (VLA), which has now merged with the AHVLA at Weybridge in Surrey, employs veterinary surgeons who carry out research and provide support for various field activities.

The Veterinary Medicines Directorate deals with the licensing of drugs.

Veterinary teaching and research

Veterinary researchers play a vital role in advancing our understanding of diseases. Research in this field enhances the health, welfare and usefulness of both food-producing and companion animals, and helps to safeguard the public from diseases. Investigations of a comparative nature also help us to understand and manage human disease, for example in cancer, genetics, reproduction and infections. The majority of research takes place at the university veterinary schools and at research institutes (which, unlike veterinary practices, are financed by the government), in laboratories and in private enterprise. Many careers in research span the interface between human and veterinary medicine, which provides a huge scope for variety in the role.

A qualification in veterinary science is more than a licence to practise. It can also open up opportunities for those interested in university teaching and research at home and overseas. In addition to clinical research work, some veterinary surgeons undergo further postgraduate training in the biological sciences. Specialisation is possible in physiology, pathology, microbiology, nutrition, genetics and statistics. Veterinary scientists are not exclusively found working in institutions concerned with animal health and disease; they can also work in natural science laboratories, medical schools and medical research institutes. The opportunities are there for young veterinary surgeons attracted by a research career.

Veterinary schools provide some of the referral hospitals to which veterinary surgeons can refer cases needing more specialised treatment. For example, recent success in the treatment of equine colic stemmed from early recognition and referral of appropriate cases allied to developments in anaesthesia and monitoring, improved surgical techniques and suture materials, plus better post-operative care. Good teamwork between the referring practitioner and the university specialists plays a big part.

Veterinary graduates are employed as research scientists by Defra, the Biotechnology and Biological Sciences Research Council, the Animal Health Trust, and in pharmaceutical and other industrial research organisations.

Case study

Mary Cecilia graduated from Nottingham University in 2012. She has been working in a veterinary surgery in Suffolk ever since.

'An office job was never for me, neither my mother or my father were in one so it never struck me as something I was keen to join. I have been working as a vet now for little over four years since graduating. Would I say it has been rewarding? Absolutely yes. Would I say it had been easy? Are you kidding me?! No, but that is what makes the job so fulfilling, every day is different and forces me to keep learning, to adapt, to discover. I am so grateful that I am in a job that offers lifelong learning.

'One of the most gratifying things is the love that the animals give you. Think of the feeling you get from your pet and it is that but with a variety of animals on a daily cycle. Not all the animals are friendly though; what is important is that you remember that they are coming to see you because there is something wrong with them, they cannot communicate that with you, therefore you need to understand that it is not personal. It certainly is not that.

'The investigative side of the job is the bit I am drawn to most. The process, the interpretation of the data, the administration of treatment, it really does enable mental stimulation. I always found the mathematics side hard though, so calculating drug dosage or similar is a little more mental stimulation that I can take at times!

'Surgery is the biggest challenge from a skills point of view. It is a very daunting feeling knowing that you hold the life of the animal in your hands, though only if you stop and think about it, which, to be brutally honest, with a trainee vet, you don't once you have done your first few surgeries. It is an integral part of the job and you would be amazed how quickly any nervousness is overridden by sharp and complete focus. Myself, I like to play classical music while concentrating, I have always believed in the studies that show that it increases alertness. I know others do it differently and I have many colleagues who have their own process.

'The hardest part of the job is the part you wish you never had to do; putting an animal to sleep. I won't dwell on this, other than to say, steel yourself as early as you can. No one says don't be empathetic, if anything it will make you a better vet if you are; the point is to separate human feeling from what is in the best interest of the animal. That is challenge number one. Challenge number two is to deal with the pet owner. My only advice is compassion is a compelling argument if an animal is suffering.

'So, I heartily promote and champion the veterinary profession. I don't think it is without its faults, or its hardships, as most professions are, however what I do think is that it is the most wonderfully diverse, gratifying process you can be part of and, as with anything, what you get out of it will be defined by what you put in. Be robust: remember there will be difficult customers. Be resilient: for there will be hard times. Be ruthless (not quite): because you are running a business at the end of the day and keeping a pet is expensive. Be rewarded: daily, by not forgetting the privileged role you are in, one where you get to help animals and people and to go to work every day doing what you most enjoy.'

New trends

Membership of the EU brought a new source of income into general practice. This was brought about through increased certification required in the interests of safeguarding public health: every abattoir had to have an official veterinary surgeon to see that it operated hygienically and that slaughtering was humane. Full-time vets were appointed to the Food

Standards Agency to ensure that ethical practice was upheld in the slaughter of animals and hygiene and food safety for the general public. Every port and airport was to have a veterinary surgeon available.

This is all past tense because of Brexit, and it is unclear at time of going to print whether this situation will remain the same and what impact that will have on wider standards as much will depend on the two-year negotiations once Article 50 has been triggered. However, there will undoubtedly be some change because, at this moment, bodies such as the BVA are part of the Federation of Veterinarians of Europe (FVE), one of 38 organisations that have a say on standards across Europe. With the UK voting to leave, there will be some renegotiation on membership no doubt. At this stage it is difficult to say and therefore students are encouraged to monitor this position in the ensuing negotiation.

Other career paths

The Army employs veterinary scientists in the Royal Army Veterinary Corps, where they care for service animals, mostly working dogs and horses used for ceremonial purposes. They also have public health responsibilities and opportunities for research or postgraduate study. Those recruited join with the rank of an Army captain for a four-year Short Service Commission, but this may be altered to a Regular Commission on application.

Some veterinary surgeons prefer to work for animal welfare societies, such as the RSPCA, PDSA and Blue Cross. Others work as inspectors for the Home Office.

Table 7 Expected annual earnings, pre bonus, add-ons and profit share (approx. and variable) – Veterinary Surgeon

Salary	Length of experience
£28,000	0–5 years
£38,400	5–10 years
£40,400	10–20 years
£41,643	>21 years

Source: www.payscale.com/research/UK/Job=Veterinarian/Salary
Reprinted with kind permission from www.payscale.com

The Society of Practising Veterinary Surgeons is now reporting that the gender pay gap has closed to within 10%, and while this is slightly higher than it is in most professions, it is definitely the sign of changing attitudes within the profession.

Veterinary nurses

Veterinary nurses work alongside veterinary surgeons and provide full support in veterinary surgeries or hospitals, ensuring the highest standard of care for the animals. Their work covers a wide range of duties, such as diagnostics (tests), treatments and minor surgery; they also are involved in major surgery, monitoring the animals while under anaesthetic. One crucial role of a veterinary nurse is education – teaching owners about animal husbandry. Veterinary nurses have good opportunities for career advancement and the longer they have worked in a particular practice, the more responsibility they will be given, for example managerial tasks such as managing teams either in a surgery or in an animal hospital. They will also be required to train new members of staff.

There are opportunities available in different environments too, such as veterinary research, universities, kennels and zoos. This can be an alternative career path for anyone who has not been able to obtain a place within a practice. The important thing to note is that there are lots of options.

In order to become a veterinary nurse, you need to train. This can either be on a vocational route or through higher education. They both allow you to register as a veterinary nurse. The vocational course is for those who prefer practical work. This Level 3 diploma can be obtained on either a full-time or a part-time basis while you work within a veterinary practice. The degree course is longer and more academic but it will open up opportunities in research in the future and in other careers, such as teaching. The latter course should be applied for via UCAS.

The standard length of a veterinary nursing course is three years but there are some institutions that offer a four-year sandwich programme, allowing you to work while training. For a course that you apply for through UCAS, the grades will be variable, but a standard offer is around 48 UCAS points at the lower end of the scale, usually a college, to 112 UCAS points at the higher end at established universities, such as Harper Adams. They often look for A level Biology at Grade C as well. There are many places that offer these courses, from colleges such as Duchy College, to Bristol University. The list of the main providers is as follows.

Askham Bryan College: Veterinary Nursing (D310); Veterinary Nursing (top-up) (D311)

University of Bristol: Veterinary Nursing and Bioveterinary Science (DC37)

Duchy College: Veterinary Nursing (D311)

Easton and Otley College (an Associate College of UEA): Vet Nursing (D310)

Edinburgh Napier University: Veterinary Nursing (D310)

Harper Adams University: Veterinary Nursing (D314); Veterinary Nursing with Companion Animal Behaviour (D313); Veterinary Nursing with Small Animal Rehabilitation (D310)

Hartpury University Centre: Equine Veterinary Nursing (Top Up) (D312); Equine Veterinary Nursing Science (D311); Veterinary Nursing Science (BD71); Veterinary Nursing Science (D310)

Kingston Maurward College: Veterinary Nursing (682F)

University of Liverpool: Foundation to Health and Veterinary Studies (Nursing) (Year 0) (Y4AS)

Middlesex University: Veterinary Nursing (D316); Veterinary Nursing (D315); Veterinary Nursing (D313)

Myerscough College: Veterinary Nursing (D313); Veterinary Nursing (Top-up) (D312)

Nottingham Trent University: Veterinary Nursing FT (D312)

Oxford Brookes University: Advanced Veterinary Nursing Studies (BSc) (D312); Advanced Veterinary Nursing Studies (FdSc) (D310)

Plumpton College: Veterinary Nursing (D310)

RVC: Veterinary Nursing (D313); Veterinary Nursing (D310)

Sheffield College: Veterinary Nursing (D3H9)

Coleg Sir Gar / Carmarthenshire College: Veterinary Nursing (2K5G)

University of South Wales: Veterinary Nursing (N231)

Sparsholt College Hampshire: Veterinary Nursing Science (D311); Veterinary Nursing Science (D310)

SRUC – Scotland's Rural College: Veterinary Nursing (4D70)

Warwickshire College Group: Veterinary Nursing (D311); Veterinary Nursing (D310); Veterinary Nursing (Top Up) (D3NF); Veterinary Physiotherapy (56D2)

College of West Anglia: Veterinary Nursing and Applied Animal Behaviour (D990); Veterinary Nursing and Applied Animal Behaviour (D391)

Writtle University College: Veterinary Physiotherapy (W4F3)

Source: www.ucas.com. We acknowledge UCAS' contribution of this information.

Women in the profession

Over three times as many women are now admitted to veterinary science courses as men. The table below shows figures from UCAS' 2016 end of year cycle applicant statistics. The figures might be rough approximations this year, but in most years the split is considered to be 80% female applicants to 20% male applicants. Therefore, gents, there is a balance to be addressed here!

Women comprise about a third of all the vets in the country, but only one in five of the sole principals in general practice are women. Two explanations have been suggested for this. One is that the statistic reflects past intakes into the profession and this is changing. Another is that, whereas women are in the majority at age 26–35, they comprise only one in five of those aged 50 or over. This suggests that they leave the profession early – perhaps in order to have a family – and do not always return. The figures also hint that women are slightly more inclined than their male colleagues to work in the public sector.

Table 8 UCAS 2016 End of Cycle applicant statistics for Pre-clinical Veterinary Medicine: male and female applicants

	All applicants	Degree accepts	Clearing accepts
Men	1,615	225	10
Women	6,320	990	50
Total	**7,935**	**1,215**	**60**

Source: www.ucas.com.

UCAS Tariff

The UCAS Tariff is used by about one third of universities in their offer conditions to students, instead of asking for specific grades. Not all universities use the Tariff and it is highly unlikely that it will be used for veterinary medicine; however, for some veterinary nursing courses, entry requirements are quoted in Tariff points. Universities are more likely to stipulate grades rather than points, mostly because the points do not necessarily equate to the grades. There is the possibility though that they might ask for grades as well as points if they are using the new Tariff, i.e. a minimum requirement in a certain subject.

The new Tariff system for the main post-16 qualifications can be calculated using Table 9 on the following page. For more information, visit the UCAS website.

Table 9 UCAS Tariff

A level	AS	IB HL	IB SL	EPQ	Pre U	Scottish Advanced Higher	Scottish Higher	Irish Leaving Certificate
A* = 56	–	7 = 56	7 = 28	A* = 28	D1 = 56	A = 56	A = 33	H1 = 36
A = 48	A = 20	6 = 48	6 =24	A = 24	D2 = 56	B = 48	B = 27	H2 = 30
B = 40	B = 16	5 = 32	5 =16	B = 20	D3 = 52	C = 40	C = 21	H3 = 24
C = 32	C = 12	4 = 24	4 =12	C = 16	M1 = 44	D =32	D =15	H4 = 18
D = 24	D = 10	3 = 12	3 =6	D = 12	M2 = 40	–	–	H5 = 12
E = 16	E = 6	–	–	E = 8	M3 = 36	–	–	H6 = 9
–	–	–	–	–	P1 = 28	–	–	–
–	–	–	–	–	P2 = 24	–	–	–
–	–	–	–	–	P3 = 20	–	–	–

Source: www.ucas.com
We acknowledge UCAS' contribution of this information. For further details of all qualifications awarded UCAS Tariff points see the UCAS website. Note that the Tariff is constantly updated and new qualifications are added every year.

Dealing with people

Being in veterinary practice means that you are running a business. This means that, for example, today's vets have to be familiar with computer records on health and know how to interpret them; but there is a more important factor: vets have to be customer oriented. Students soon pick this up. 'The way we approach people is crucial; it's our bread and butter,' remarked one vet. 'It's the same on the telephone. We make a point of being cheerful and reassuring with a few words of advice until we can get there.' This aspect of practice is now so important that some practices hire a manager to run the administrative side and help to train reception staff.

The professional approach

With increasing professionalism and rising customer expectations come higher overheads. While training, it is vital that a student realises the importance of everything that makes up a surgery. The establishment and maintenance of a modern veterinary surgery now require a considerable capital sum of money, so most newly qualified vets will start their career by going into practice with other vets. The most ambitious vet will aspire to and attain a partnership after two or three surgery moves; a few, after gaining experience over three or four years, will branch out on their own. Appreciating this route is imperative for a vet because it helps you to map out your own career path; if you can understand what is required when working in practice, you can see what is essential and integral and this will help to shape your approach to your career and perhaps to a future surgery. Most courses now make some attempt to introduce the student to the economics of running a practice, although, as one vet commented wryly: 'Few will think of bookkeeping!'

Summing up

Many students are interested in becoming veterinary surgeons. For some it will remain a pipe dream either because they lack the ability or skill, or because their ideas about being a veterinary surgeon are not rooted in reality. However, there are real opportunities for those who are motivated and determined to reach their goal. The competition is intense but not impossible, and prospective students should be encouraged to explore the veterinary option early by seeking practical experience. As one vet put it: 'See a farm, get your wellies dirty, experience some blood and gore, and see that the life of a vet is not all about cuddly puppies!' This will test both resolve and suitability.

The demand for veterinary services and research-related activities is strong and is increasing. Market forces do dictate the number of places in veterinary schools, but funding limitations imposed by the higher education funding councils are also a controlling factor. Nevertheless, the profession of veterinary surgeon retains its popularity among young people. It is not because of the money, the car, or accommodation – which is often next to the practice, ready for instant call-outs. Nor can the hours be the attraction: the provision of a 24-hour service to the public is mandatory. Rather, it is probably the sense that being a vet is a way of life rather than a job.

As we have been discussing, however, there is expected to be a significant impact of the Brexit vote on the veterinary profession, in terms of education, regulation and workforce planning. It is likely to also have an effect on research, surveillance, animal movements and animal welfare. However, time will tell the impact and much will be clearer as the negotiations unfold over the next two years.

The unique skills a vet requires

An experienced vet operating a mixed practice on the Wirral put the unique qualities of being a vet this way: 'I think people respect what we do. Every Friday a lady brings us a chocolate cake. It's little things like this that make you feel appreciated.' A vet is many things – skilled surgeon, business manager, counsellor and confidant. Vets know that their animals are often the most important thing in their clients' lives. They have tremendous responsibility for the animals, whether in sickness or in health, and when all other options have failed they have the authority and power vested in them by law to take the animal's life. They devote their lives to animal welfare but their role is not based on sentimentality. Find out whether it is the life for you, and, if it is, go for it.

Fact: Horses can't vomit.

12| Don't count your chickens before they've hatched
Further information

Do not ever make the mistake of believing that you know enough, because you can always find out more. If you want to be the cat that got the cream, do your research. You will be more likely to get in to your first choice of university if you do your own investigations about where you want to go.

Remember, there is no harm in entering into a dialogue with an admissions tutor if you are asking pertinent and considered questions. An elephant never forgets and neither does an admissions tutor.

Listed below are the contact details of the veterinary schools in the UK and websites of other organisations that might help your research.

Veterinary schools in the UK

Bristol
Department of Clinical Veterinary Science
University of Bristol
Langford House
Langford BS40 5DU
Tel (veterinary admissions): 0117 394 1641
Email: bristol-ug@bristol.ac.uk
Website: www.bristol.ac.uk/vetscience

Cambridge
Veterinary Admission Enquiries Adviser
Department of Veterinary Medicine
University of Cambridge
Madingley Road
Cambridge CB3 0ES
Tel: 01223 330811
Email: admissions.enquiries@vet.cam.ac.uk
Website: www.vet.cam.ac.uk

Edinburgh
The Admissions Officer
Royal (Dick) School of Veterinary Studies
University of Edinburgh
Easter Bush Campus
Midlothian EH25 9RG
Tel: 0131 651 7305
Email: vetug@ed.ac.uk
Website: www.ed.ac.uk/vet

Glasgow
Admissions Office
School of Veterinary Medicine
College of Medical, Veterinary and Life Sciences
University of Glasgow
Garscube Campus
Bearsden Road
Glasgow G61 1QH
Tel: 0141 330 2225
Email: reception@vet.gla.ac.uk
Website: www.gla.ac.uk/schools/vet

Liverpool
Admissions Sub-Dean
School of Veterinary Science
Thompson Yates Building
University of Liverpool
Liverpool L69 3GB
Tel: 0151 794 4797
Email: vetadmit@liverpool.ac.uk
Website: www.liv.ac.uk/veterinary-science/

London
The Registry
Royal Veterinary College
University of London
Royal College Street
London NW1 0TU
Tel: 020 7468 5147
Email: admissions@rvc.ac.uk
Website: www.rvc.ac.uk

Nottingham
Admissions Team
School of Veterinary Medicine and Science
University of Nottingham
Sutton Bonington Campus
College Road
Sutton Bonington LE12 5RD

Tel: 0115 951 6464
Email: veterinary-enquiries@nottingham.ac.uk
Website: www.nottingham.ac.uk/vet

Surrey
School of Veterinary Medicine
Faculty of Health and Medical Sciences
Vet School Main Building (VSM)
University of Surrey
Daphne Jackson Road
Guildford
Surrey GU2 7AL
Tel: 01483 683882
Email: vetschool@surrey.ac.uk

Other contacts and sources of information

Useful organisations and websites

- **Animal Welfare Foundation:** www.bva-awf.org.uk
- **Blue Cross:** www.bluecross.org.uk
- **British Equine Veterinary Association:** www.beva.org.uk
- **British Veterinary Association** (this is the national representative body for the British veterinary profession): www.bva.co.uk
- **Department for Environment, Food and Rural Affairs (Defra):** www.defra.gov.uk
- **Mander Portman Woodward:** www.mpw.ac.uk
- **People's Dispensary for Sick Animals:** www.pdsa.org.uk

Royal College of Veterinary Surgeons
Belgravia House
62–64 Horseferry Road
London SW1P 2AF
Tel: 020 7222 2001 / General enquiries: 020 7202 0791
Email: education@rcvs.org.uk
Website: www.rcvs.org.uk

St George's University
University Centre
Grenada
West Indies
Tel: 0800 169 9061 ext. 1413
Email: sguenrolment@sgu.edu
Website: www.sgu.edu

University of Medicine in Kosice, Slovak Republic
Recruitment (XLNC)
Application to Faculty of Medicine
UPJS in Kosice

Matuskova 18
Trieda SNP 1
04011 Kosice
Slovak Republic
Tel: +42 155 234 3319
Email: info@medicinekosice.eu; nela.farkasova@upjs.sk;
lenka.radaciova@upjs.sk (Applicants)
Website: www.upjs.sk/en/facility-of-medicine/

Society of Practising Veterinary Surgeons
www.spvs.org.uk
Provides advice to veterinary surgeons.

Universities and Colleges Admissions Service
www.ucas.com

Vet Times
www.vettimes.co.uk
Online database and resource.

GOV.UK
www.gov.uk/student-finance
Information on student loans and grants.

The Department of Agriculture and Rural Development (Northern Ireland)
www.dardni.gov.uk

The Student Room
www.thestudentroom.co.uk

Member of the Royal College of Veterinary Surgeons
www.mrcvs.co.uk

WikiVet
https://en.wikivet.net/Veterinary_Education_Online

World Organisation for Animal Health
www.oie.int/animal-health-in-the-world/oie-listed-diseases-2016

Courses

VetCam
Tel: 01223 330811
Two-day residential 'Introduction to Veterinary Science in Cambridge' course, held in March.

Vetsim
www.workshop-uk.net/vetsim
Conference organised by Workshop Conferences for interested sixth-formers and held annually in Nottingham.

Publications

Getting into Oxford & Cambridge: 2018 Entry (publication date April 2017), Lucy Bates, Trotman Education.
Packed with essential advice to help you win one of the fiercely sought-after places at Oxbridge, this guide tells you everything you need to know to make a successful application. Featuring case studies from current students throughout, it also gives an insight into what studying at Oxford and Cambridge is really like.

HEAP 2018: University Degree Course Offers, 48th edition (publication date May 2017), Brian Heap, Trotman Education.
Lists the target offers and admissions details for over 100 main degree subjects at universities and colleges across the UK, helping applicants to choose the right course and win their place.

How to Complete Your UCAS Application: 2018 Entry, 29th edition (publication date May 2017), Beryl Dixon, Trotman Education.
Works through the application procedure step by step using examples, and includes information on how to avoid the most common mistakes and how to write a winning personal statement.

Glossary

Admissions tutor
The person in charge of your application.

American Veterinary Medical Association (AVMA)
The AVMA represents US veterinarians, providing information, publications and resources such as training courses.

Animal Health and Veterinary Laboratories Agency (AHVLA)
Working on behalf of Defra throughout Great Britain, the AHVLA was established to ensure animal health and welfare and public health.

Animal husbandry
An agricultural term meaning breeding and raising livestock.

Bachelor of Veterinary Medicine (BVetMed)
A bachelor's degree for studies in the United Kingdom. Most courses are five years in length, although Cambridge has a six-year course and chooses to award a Bachelor of Arts (BA) after three years, followed by a Bachelor of Veterinary Medicine (VetMB) after six years.

BioMedical Admissions Test (BMAT)
This examination is taken by students looking to apply for veterinary medicine at the University of Cambridge.

Bovine spongiform encephalopathy (BSE)
Commonly referred to as mad cow disease, BSE is a neurological disease that affects the brains of cattle. The human form of the disease is Creutzfeldt–Jakob disease (CJD).

Bovine tuberculosis (bTB)
Bovine tuberculosis is a serious disease in cattle. It is said to be commonly spread by badgers, which are a protected species, and therefore the debate remains over whether badgers should be culled.

British Equine Veterinary Association (BEVA)
The BEVA is the leading body for the equine veterinary profession. It ensures high standards throughout the profession, has 2,400 members globally and also runs outstanding continuing professional development (CPD) courses.

Clinical years
The third and fourth years of veterinary medicine degree courses.

Continuing professional development (CPD)
The Royal College of Veterinary Surgeons' Code of Professional Conduct for Veterinary Surgeons states that veterinary surgeons have a responsibility to 'maintain and develop the knowledge and skills relevant to their professional practice and competence'. A minimum amount of 105 hours over an ongoing three-year period is recommended for CPD, with an average of 35 hours per year.

Department for Environment, Food and Rural Affairs (Defra)
The government department that looks after environmental protection, agriculture, food production standards, fisheries and rural communities in the United Kingdom. It is responsible for maintaining high standards within the industries.

Department of Agriculture and Rural Development (DARDNI)
For information on veterinay medicine in Northern Ireland.

European Association of Establishments for Veterinary Education (EAEVE)
The EAEVE aims to harmonise the standards of veterinary tuition in the European Union, giving confidence to members of the public and veterinary professionals.

Extramural rotations (EMR)
EMR are undertaken by students studying at veterinary school; the time is divided between farming work and experience in veterinary practice.

Extramural studies (EMS)
EMS are studies that take place outside the university setting. The Royal College of Veterinary Surgeons states that students must complete 38 weeks of EMS during their course: 12 weeks of pre-clinical and 26 weeks of clinical placements.

Foot-and-mouth disease (FMD)
FMD is a viral disease that affects cattle, pigs, sheep, goats and deer. Hedgehogs and rats can also become infected, and people, cats, dogs and game animals can carry infected material. FMD is more contagious than any other animal disease, and the mortality rate among young animals is high.

Fresher
A first-year undergraduate student.

FVE
Federation of Veterinarians of Europe.

Integrated course
A course that teaches lots of different disciplines which all come together in the final year of study. The individual elements are taught by specialists in disciplines ranging from pharmacology to anatomy.

International English Language Testing System (IELTS)
An English test used to determine the level of language ability for international students. A typical score of 7.0 is required.

Intramural rotations (IMR)
IMR take place in the clinical years of veterinary medicine, and are designed to develop and utilise skills you have previously learnt. You will work in clinical teams and have access to clinical records. This will encourage you to present a professional image.

Master of Science (MSc)
The MSc is typically a taught programme over one or two years, depending on the university.

Methicillin-resistant *Staphylococcus aureus* (MRSA)
MRSA, commonly known as the 'superbug', is a human-based infection found in hospitals but it can also colonise and cause infections in pets and farm animals.

Multiple choice questions (MCQs)
MCQs are used in some veterinary examinations.

North American Veterinary Licensing Examination (NAVLE)
In order to practise in North America, students must pass the NAVLE.

People's Dispensary for Sick Animals (PDSA)
The PDSA is a veterinary charity that offers healthcare for a range of animals.

Pharmacodynamics
The study of the mechanism of the action of drugs and how they affect the body.

Pharmacokinetics
The study of the absorption, distribution, metabolism and excretion of drugs.

Pre-clinical years
The first two years of veterinary medicine.

Professional Development Phase (PDP)
The first year after completing your degree is the PDP, when you are expected to develop your skills.

Royal College of Veterinary Surgeons (RCVS)
The regulatory body for all veterinary professionals in the United Kingdom. The RCVS's role is to ensure the health and welfare of animals and the efficient practice of veterinary professionals and to provide an impartial opinion on animal health and disease as well as on the latest debates.

Royal Society for the Prevention of Cruelty to Animals (RSPCA)
The leading UK charity specialising in the care, control and rescue of animals.

Royal Veterinary College (RVC)
The oldest and largest of the veterinary schools in the United Kingdom and one of the world's leading specialist veterinary schools.

Therapeutics
The use of drugs in the prevention and treatment of disease.

Universities and Colleges Admissions Service (UCAS)
The central body through which students apply to veterinary schools; you do not apply to the universities directly. You can choose four veterinary courses and one non-veterinary course.

Veterinary Laboratories Agency (VLA)
Centre set up to operate and support control schemes in the interests of public health, to monitor developments and give early warning of any disease problems or dangers to the safety of the food chain; now part of the Animal Health and Veterinary Laboratories Agency.

Veterinary Medicines Directorate (VMD)
The VMD deals with the licensing of drugs.

Fact: 'The quick brown fox jumps over a lazy dog' – it does this while using every letter of the alphabet.